teach yourself

spanish
vocabulary

teach yourself ®

spanish
vocabulary
mike zollo
series editor
rosi mcnab

For UK order enquiries: please contact Bookpoint Ltd, 130 Milton Park, Abingdon, Oxon OX14 4SB. Telephone: +44 (0) 1235 827720. Fax: +44 (0) 1235 400454. Lines are open 09.00–18.00, Monday to Saturday, with a 24-hour message answering service. Details about our titles and how to order are available at www.teachyourself.co.uk.

For USA order enquiries: please contact McGraw-Hill Customer Services, PO Box 545, Blacklick, OH 43004-0545, USA. Telephone: 1-800-722-4726. Fax: 1-614-755-5645.

For Canada order enquiries: please contact McGraw-Hill Ryerson Ltd, 300 Water St, Whitby, Ontario L1N 9B6, Canada. Telephone: 905 430 5000. Fax: 905 430 5020.

Long renowned as the authoritative source for self-guided learning – with more than 30 million copies sold worldwide – the *Teach Yourself* series includes over 300 titles in the fields of languages, crafts, hobbies, business, computing and education.

British Library Cataloguing in Publication Data: a catalogue entry for this title is available from The British Library.

Library of Congress Catalog Card Number: on file.

First published in UK 2003 by Hodder Headline Ltd, 338 Euston Road, London NW1 3BH.

First published in US 2003 by Contemporary Books, a division of the McGraw Hill Companies, 1 Prudential Plaza, 130 East Randolph Street, Chicago, Illinois 60601 USA.

The 'Teach Yourself' name is a registered trade mark of Hodder & Stoughton Ltd.

Typeset by Transet Limited, Coventry, England.
Printed in Great Britain for Hodder & Stoughton Educational, a division of Hodder Headline Ltd, 338 Euston Road, London NW1 3BH, by Cox & Wyman Ltd, Reading, Berkshire.

Papers used in this book are natural, renewable and recyclable products. They are made from wood grown in sustainable forests. The logging and manufacturing processes conform to the environmental regulations of the country of origin.

Impression number   10 9 8 7 6 5 4 3 2
Year   2009 2008 2007 2006 2005 2004 2003

contents

There have been many studies carried out into the way we learn vocabulary. The Swiss, who are generally acknowledged as experts in multi-language learning are also leaders in the understanding of the processes of language acquisition and some of their findings may be of interest to people wanting to broaden their vocabulary.

> Studies have shown that the most successful way [of learning vocabulary] is when the student is able to relate the new word to a concept and to integrate it into a conceptual system.
>
> (Wokusch, 1997)

Put simply this means that the most successful way of learning vocabulary is to put the new language into a context.

When a child first learns a language they are learning the concepts as well as the language at the same time. If you give a child an ice cream and say 'ice cream' they are learning the word and the concept at the same time, associating the word and the object. An adult has the advantage of already having the concept. An ice cream already conjures up other words: cold, vanilla, strawberry, like, don't like, size, price, etc.

Similarly if you decide to learn about a computer or a car you probably already know the parts or expressions you want to learn and can visualize them before you meet the word. In fact you already have the 'concept' and you can 'place' the new words within that concept.

It is for this reason that the vocabulary in this book has been given in context rather than, as in a dictionary, in alphabetical order. The words have been chosen as the words most likely to be useful or of interest to the learner.

One of the most useful tips in learning a new language is to look for ways of remembering a word: find a 'hook' to hang your new word or phrase on.

How this book works

This book is more than just a list of words – it is a key to open the door to better communication. It is designed to give you the confidence you need to communicate better in Spanish by increasing your knowledge of up-to-date vocabulary and at the same time showing you how to use the new words you are learning.

The first part of the book includes some useful learning tips, rules on pronunciation and shortcuts to look out for when learning new words. The toolbox provides you with the tools you need to speak a language. It includes basic information about the structure of the language and useful tips, including how to address people, how to ask questions, how to talk about what you have done and what you are going to do, useful expressions, and shortcuts to language learning. This part of the book is designed to be used for general reference.

The main part of the book is divided into topic areas: personal matters, family, work, education, etc. The selected words are the ones which our research has shown are the ones which are likely to be the most useful or most relevant to the learner of today. The words have been carefully arranged, grouped with other related words, nouns, verbs, adjectives etc. and useful expressions with up-to-date notes about language fashions where relevant, so that the new language can be used immediately.

Make learning a list of words more interesting

- First decide which list you are going to look at today.
- See how many words you know already and tick them off.
- Choose which new words you want to learn – don't try to do too many at once!
- Count them so you know how many you are going to try to learn.
- Say them aloud; you could even record yourself saying them.

Remembering new words

- Try to associate new words with words that sound similar in English: **plato** (*plateau*).
- Try to associate the words with pictures or situations, e.g. try to imagine a picture of a rose when you say the word: *rosa*
- See if you can split the word into bits, some of which you know already: **super-mercado**.
- Look for words related to ones you know already: **día** (*day*), **diario** (*daily newspaper*); **zapato** (*shoe*), **zapatería** (*shoe shop*)
- Look for words related to the English ones: **mano** (*manual*); **bicicleta** (*bicycle*).
- Learn the value of typical beginnings and endings used to alter the meaning of words: **<u>des</u>honesto** (<u>*dis*</u>*honest*), **<u>im</u>posible** (<u>*im*</u>*possible*), **independ<u>encia</u>** (*independ<u>ence</u>*), **capacid<u>ad</u>** (*capacit<u>y</u>*).
- Copy a list of the most important words onto A4 paper with a broad felt tip; stick it on the wall so that you can study it when doing some routine activity such as washing up, ironing, shaving or putting on make-up.
- For names of objects around the house, you could write the word on a sticky label or post-it note and attach it to the actual object.
- Copy lists of words in Spanish and English in two columns. First, say each word aloud, then cover up one column, and try to remember each word in the other column.
- Do something else for half an hour and then come back and see how many you can still remember.
- Write down the first letter of each new word and put a dot for each missing letter, cover the word up and see if you can complete the word.
- Pick a few words you find difficult to remember: write each one down with the letters jumbled up; leave them for a while, then later try to unscramble each one.
- In your list, mark the difficult words: ask someone else to test you on the ones you have marked.

Spelling tips

These don't always work but they may help!

- Words which begin with **esc**, **esp** or **est** – take off the **e**: **escalar** (*to scale, climb*); **España** (*Spain*); **estudiante** (*student*).
- Words beginning with **ll** – try *cl*, *fl* or *pl*: **llama** (*flame*); **llano** (*plain*).

- If a word begins with **f** + a vowel, try *ph*: **farmacia** (*pharmacy*)
- If a word begins with **t**, try *th*: **teatro** – *theatre*.
- Where you see a word with the letters **ie** in the middle, try replacing them with just **e**: **prefiero** (*I prefer*); **diez** (*ten*, related to decimal).
- Where you see a word with the letters **ue** in the middle, try replacing them with *o*: **puerto** (*port*).
- Words which begin with **con-**, **dis-**, **im-**, **in-**, **re-**, **sub-** in Spanish usually begin with *con-*, *dis-*, *im-*, *in-*, *re-*, *sub-* in English; words beginning with **des-** in Spanish begin with *dis-* in English.
- Many words which end in **-able** and **-ible** in Spanish usually have the same ending in English; other similar English-Spanish endings are:

Spanish	-ero/-era, -or/-ora	-miento	-aje	-oso/a	-ista	-ción	-al
English	-er	-ment	-age	-ous	-ist	-tion	-al

Write words down

Short cuts: looking for patterns

Certain letter patterns reveal important facts about the type of word you are trying to learn.

- Most words in Spanish ending in **-o** (except verbs) are masculine, belonging to the same group of words as real masculine words such as **chico** (*boy*) and **toro** (*bull*)
- Most words in Spanish ending in **-a** (except verbs) are feminine, belonging to the same group of words as real feminine words such as **chica** (*girl*) and **vaca** (*cow*)
- Most masculine words end in **-o**.
- Most feminine words end in **-a**.
- Words ending in **-aje**, **-or**, and **-án** are masculine.
- Words ending in **-ión**, **-dad** are feminine.
- Almost all verb forms end in a vowel, **s** or **n**, **r** or **d**: -a, -e, -i, -o; -as, -es, -áis, -éis, ís, -mos; -an, -en, -ron, -rán; -ar, -er, -ir; -ad, -ed, -id.

Other patterns can be seen in Spanish which are similar to those in English:

- Words ending in **-mente** (adverbs) are similar to English words ending in **-ly**, such as **rápidamente** (*rapidly*);

normalmente (*normally*); as you can see, in Spanish and English they are based on adjectives, in this case **rápido** (*rapid*) and **normal** (*normal*), simply with the endings -**mente** and -**ly**.

- Sometimes if you know a basic Spanish word, it is easy to work out an adapted version. Here are some examples showing how this works:

-ero	= *-er*	**granja** (*farm*), **granjero** (*farmer*)
-or	= *-er*	**conducir** (*to drive*), **conductor** (*driver*)
-oso/a	= *-ous*	**fábula** (*fable*), **fabuloso** (*fabulous*)
-ista	= *-ist*	**guitarra** (*guitar*), **guitarrista** (*guitarist*)

- Similarly, some Spanish words can be converted by adding a syllable at the beginning, and most work the same as in English, as follows:

con-	= *con-*	**tener** (*to have, hold*), **contener** (*to contain implies within*)
re-	= *re-*	**inventar** (*to invent*), **reinventar** (*to reinvent*)

- the following syllables added to the beginning of a word cause it to have the opposite or negative meaning:

dis-/des-	= *dis-*	**aparecer** (*to appear*), **desaparecer** (*to disappear*)
im-	= *im-*	**posible** (*possible*), **imposible** (*impossible*)
in-	= *in-*	**tolerante** (*tolerant*), **intolerante** (*intolerant*)

The alphabet

This is the English alphabet with Spanish pronunciation, which is useful if you need to spell out your name, surname, address and so on. The letters peculiar to the Spanish alphabet are listed separately at the end.

a	**a** as in **cat**
b	**be** as in **berry**
c	**the** as in **the**spian (soft)
d	**de** as in **den**, or **the** as in **the**n
e	**e** as in **egg**
f	**efe** as in **ef**fective

g   je – rough h sound as in clearing your throat
h   **atche**
i   ee as in p**ee**p
j   **hota** starting with rough **h** sound
k   **ca** as in **ca**t
l   **ele** as in **el**ephant
m   **eme** as in **em**ery board
n   **ene** as in **en**emy
o   **o** as in c**o**t
p   **pe** as in **pe**ar
q   **cu** as in **cu**ckoo
r   **erre** as in he**r**etic, with rolled r
s   **ese** as in **es**sence
t   **te** as in **te**rrible
u   **oo** as in cuck**oo**
v   **oove**: **oo** as in cuck**oo** and **e** as in **e** above
w   **oovedoble**: **oove** as in the above, plus **dobblei**
x   **eckeess**
y   **ee griyega** (Greek **i**)
z   **theta** as in **the**spian

The following are letters peculiar to the Spanish alphabet, though only ñ appears separately in the dictionary.

ch   **che** as in **ch**erry
ll   **ellye**
ñ   **enye**

In addition, you may need to say some of the following if you have to spell out something more complicated:

punctuation	la puntuación
full stop	el punto final
comma	la coma
colon	dos puntos
semi colon	punto y coma
question mark	el signo de interrogación
exclamation mark	el signo de admiración
inverted commas	comillas
capital letter	la mayúscula
small letter, lower case	la minúscula
hyphen	el guión
paragraph	el párrafo
sentence	la frase
line	la línea
dash	la raya
dot-dot-dot	los puntos suspensivos

full stop, new sentence	punto y seguido
full stop, new paragraph/line	punto y aparte
next word	a continuación
space	el espacio
blank	el espacio
forward slash	la barra oblicua
backward slash	la barra inversa
@/at	la arroba
computer keyboard	el teclado
control	la tecla Control
alt	la tecla Alt
delete	la tecla de borrado, de supresión
enter	la tecla Entrar-Retorno
return	la tecla de retorno

Pronunciation

If you wish to speak Spanish with a good accent, the following tips will be useful.

1 Vowels: all are pure and always sound the same (see **the alphabet** on p. 5). Where two or more vowels occur together, each is pronounced with its normal value and in the correct order.

---

b**ue**nos d**ía**s = b**ooe**nos d**eea**s
ad**ió**s, hasta l**ue**go = ad**eeo**s, hasta l**ooe**go

---

2 Consonants are **always** pronounced, with one notable exception: **h**, which is never pronounced. Most of the consonants are pronounced as indicated in **the alphabet** on p. 6, but note that some have sounds which are different from English.

3 Note and learn the pronunciation of the following consonants:

---

	c: hard **c** before **a**, **o** and **u**: **c**asa, **c**omo, **c**ulebra
BUT:	soft **th** (**ceceo**) before **e** and **i**: **c**ero, do**c**e, **c**ine, vi**c**io (pronounced the same as **z, but** replaced by **seseo** (**s** sound) in Southern Spain and all of Latin America)
	g: hard **g** before **a**, **o** and **u**: **g**ato, **g**orra, **g**uerra
BUT:	rough **h** sound before **e** and **i**: **g**eneral, **G**inebra (this is pronounced the same as **j**)

- In verb forms, to preserve hard **c** sound, the **c** is changed to **qu** before **e**: e.g. sacar → sa**qu**é;
- Similarly, to preserve hard **g** before **e** and **i**, Spanish inserts a **u** to protect the **g**: cargar → car**gu**é
- Also, note that **z** is often used for the soft **th** sound where verb forms would otherwise affect the **c**, and **j** replaces **g** where necessary.

    hacer→ hizo

    coger → cojo

4 Note the following consonants and combinations of consonants and their pronunciation.

---

cc – as in a**cc**ión: pronounced as a**cth**ión
ll – as in **ll**ave and ca**ll**e, pronounced as -**ly**-
nn – each **n** is pronounced with normal value
rr – pronounced as a double trill of the tongue
    (compare pe**r**o and pe**rr**o)
ch – pronounced as in English: **ch**ico, azaba**ch**e

---

5 Finally, an extra hint:

---

q is always followed by **u**, which are pronounced as **k**
    que = **k**e; NEVER as in English **qu**ick

---

6 Spanish intonation: the voice rises towards a comma, and towards the end of a question, but falls towards the end of a statement.

7 Stress: all words of more than one syllable have one syllable stressed more than the rest. There are three hard and fast rules, but it is worth learning each new words with its stress pattern:

---

1 Words ending with a **vowel, n** or **s** have the stress on the **last but one** syllable.

    niño, **ha**cen, con**se**jo, diccio**na**rio, pose**sio**nes

2 Words ending with a **consonant except n** or **s** have the stress on the **last** syllable.

    Mad**rid**, mu**jer**, pa**pel**, re**loj**, cono**cer**, desayu**nar**

3 Words which break rules 1 and 2 have a **written accent** to show where the stress falls.

    mi**ró**, cham**pán**, **pá**jaro, condi**ción**, cham**pú**, ha**céis**

- When a word gains a syllable when made plural, an accent may either be lost or gained to keep the stress in the right place.

    condici**ón** → condici**ones**
    auto**bús** → auto**buses**
    ex**amen** → ex**ámenes**

Needless to say, this happens a great deal with verb forms.

- Accents are also used to distinguish between pairs of otherwise identical words.

you (object)	te	té	*tea*
your	tu	tú	*you* (subject)
if	si	sí	*yes*

To sum up, once you are familiar with all of the above rules, Spanish spelling and pronunciation are very reliable. Of course you won't learn them overnight, and it may be best to concentrate on learning and practising one at a time. Another useful method is to record and listen to spoken Spanish as often as possible. Here are some ideas as to how you can make recordings of natural spoken Spanish:

- Take a portable cassette player and some blank cassettes every time you go to Spain. Try recording from the local radio, or even people speaking, though you ought to ask their permission first!
- Try playing around with your radio tuner to find a Spanish radio station, and if you do, try to record some Spanish.
- If you have Spanish friends, ask them to make recordings for you, perhaps sending you messages with their family news, or giving their views on topics of interest to you.
- If you have satellite TV, see if you can also receive Spanish radio, and if not, talk to your local TV shop to ask if it is worth re-tuning your satellite equipment.
- If you have access to the internet, try to find Spanish radio broadcasts, which are sometimes possible via radio station websites.
- Once you have some recordings, listen to them as often as possible, and try to repeat what you hear, imitating the sounds, and repeating short chunks of Spanish. You might try writing out small sections, saying them aloud and comparing your version with the original.

- If you have Spanish friends, try recording short messages on cassette, send them to your friends, and ask them to comment on, and correct your pronunciation.
- When speaking direct to Spanish people, ask them to correct your pronunciation when possible.

toolbox

Nouns – gender and plurals

All Spanish nouns – names of things or people – are either masculine or feminine, as explained on p. 4. Most end in -o (masculine) or -a (feminine), though there are exceptions to this rule and there are also other common masculine and feminine endings. However, all nouns form their plural by adding -s or, if the noun ends in a consonant, adding -es. Adjectives behave in exactly the same way – see Section C.

libro / libros	book / books
rosa / rosas	rose / roses
coche (m) / coches	car / cars
llave (f) / llaves	key / keys
reloj / relojes	watch / watches

Many nouns, notably those referring to people, have specific masculine and feminine forms. Some of these have been used in the following table to show typical masculine, feminine, singular and plural forms:

masculine singular	feminine singular	masculine plural	feminine plural
chico *boy*	chica *girl*	chicos *boys*	chicas *girls*
hijo *son*	hija *daughter*	hijos *sons*	hijas *daughters*
hermano *brother*	hermana *sister*	hermanos *brothers*	hermanas *sisters*
tío *uncle*	tía *aunt*	tíos *uncles*	tías *aunts*
secretario *secretary*	secretaria *secretary*	secretarios *secretaries*	secretarias *secretaries*
estudiante *student*	estudiante *student*	estudiantes *students*	estudiantes *students*
profesor *teacher*	profesora *teacher*	profesores *teachers*	profesoras *teachers*

Articles and other determiners

Nouns are often preceded by an article, in English either *the* (definite article) or *a / an* (indefinite article). There are more articles in Spanish, because there are masculine, feminine, singular and plural forms as set out below. It is very useful to learn nouns with their definite or indefinite article, so that you know its gender:

un libro	*a book*	el libro / los libros	*the book / books*
una rosa	*a rose*	la rosa / las rosas	*the rose / roses*
un coche	*a car*	el coche / los coches	*the car / cars*
un reloj	*a watch*	el reloj / los relojes	*the watch / watches*

Of course, nouns can have other so-called 'determiners' (modifying words) in front of them, expressing possession or specifying which of two or more is referred to. Notice how, in the following table, nouns, articles and determiners are set out in columns: whichever column the noun is in, you can only use it with articles and determiners from that same column, so that they match the noun in gender and number (for example, **nuestra madre**). The table also includes a couple of adjectives (*old*, *young*) to show how they fit into this pattern.

meaning	masculine singular	feminine singular	masculine plural	feminine plural
child / children	niño	niña	niños	niñas
father(s) + mother(s)	padre	madre	padres	madres
old	viejo	vieja	viejos	viejas
young	joven	joven	jóvenes	jóvenes
the	el	la	los	las
a/an; some (in plural)	un	una	unos	unas
my	mi	mi	mis	mis
your (familiar)	tu	tu	tus	tus
his / her / its / your (formal)	su	su	sus	sus
our	nuestro	nuestra	nuestros	nuestras
your	vuestro	vuestra	vuestros	vuestras
their	su	su	sus	sus
this / these	este	esta	estos	estas
that / those	ese	esa	esos	esas
that / those	aquel	aquella	aquellos	aquellas

Here are some more examples:

No es mi amigo – es tu amigo.	*He's not my friend, he's yours.*
Nuestros hijos jóvenes van a esta escuela.	*Our young children go to this school.*
No me gusta este vestido; prefiero aquella falda.	*I don't like this dress; I prefer that skirt.*

Adjectives

Adjectives are describing words which add information about nouns. They have to match the noun in gender and number, so they also follow the pattern set out in the previous table. Thus, in masculine form most adjectives end in -o, and in feminine form most end in -a. Adjectives that end in -e can be used either with a masculine or a feminine noun without change; there are several other possible adjective endings. All adjectives form their plural by adding -s or -es, just as for nouns.

Unlike English, Spanish usually places adjectives just after the noun they describe, but a few can go in front. They can also be used in other situations, such as after the verb *to be*.

el jardín grande   *the large garden*
la casa pequeña   *the small house*
los melones baratos   *the cheap melons*
las bicicletas caras   *the expensive bikes*
el chico es gordo   *the boy is fat*
las manzanas son deliciosas   *the apples are delicious*

The table on page 12 shows how a couple of adjectives fit into the pattern of possible forms for nouns, adjectives, articles and determiners.

It is worth learning a few set phrases to help you remember the need for agreement and some typical endings:

masc. singular: un toro negro; el río grande; este libro interesante; tu viejo amigo
fem. singular: una paloma blanca; la isla bonita; esa chica guapa; nuestra tía tonta
masc. plural: unos vinos tintos; los ángeles buenos; aquellos chicos malos; mis hijos feos
fem. plural: unas mujeres elegantes; las vegas fértiles; estas peras maduras; sus casas modernas

Here is a list of useful adjectives for describing people; remember, those ending in -o change to -a for the feminine form, and all add -s for the plural; one or two are invariable (inv.), i.e. the same form is used for masculine and feminine forms:

tall / big	alto	*short*	bajo
thin	delgado	*fat*	gordo
old	viejo / anciano	*young*	joven
happy (contented)	contento	*sad*	triste
happy (nature)	feliz	*unhappy*	infeliz
quiet / shy	tímido	*loud*	extrovertido
relaxed / laid back	relajado	*stressed*	estresado
nice, pleasant	simpático	*nasty*	antipático
kind	amable	*unhelpful*	poco amable
self-centred / egoistic	egoísta (inv.)	*considerate / helpful*	atento
sporty / active	deportista (inv.)	*lazy*	perezoso
good looking	guapo / hermoso	*ugly*	feo
outstanding / exceptional	extraordinario	*ordinary / unremarkable*	ordinario
smart	elegante	*scruffy*	descuidado
well-behaved	que se porta bien	*naughty*	travieso
polite	cortés, educado	*rude*	grosero

The following adjectives can be used to describe things:

old	viejo	*new*	nuevo
good	bueno	*bad*	malo
cheap	barato	*expensive*	caro
fast	rápido	*slow*	lento
in good condition	en buen estado	*damaged*	en mal estado
flimsy	poco sólido	*solid*	sólido
rough	áspero	*smooth*	liso
shiny	brillante	*matt*	mate
nice	agradable	*horrible*	horrible
soft	blando	*hard*	duro
interesting	interesante	*boring*	aburrido, pesado

Often, we use adjectives to compare one thing or person with another, or with all others. To say something is ...-*er* than another, we use the comparative form of the adjective, and to say it is the ...-*est*, we use the superlative form. The comparative of most Spanish adjectives is formed by simply putting *más* in front of the adjective, and the superlative uses **el / la / los / las más** in front of the adjective. Some examples can be seen in the following table. Four Spanish adjectives – for *big, small, good* and *bad* – have different forms in the comparative and superlative, and these are shown at the end of the table. However, please note that in practice **más grande** or **más pequeño** etc. are often used instead of **mayor** or **menor** etc.

adjective		comparative		superlative	
big	grande, grandes	*bigger*	mayor mayores	*biggest*	el / la mayor los/las mayores
small	pequeño/a pequeños/as	*smaller*	menor menores	*smallest*	el / la menor los/las menores
good	bueno/a buenos/as	*better*	mejor mejores	*best*	el/la mejor los/las mejores
bad	malo/a malos/malas	*worse*	peor peores	*worse*	el/la peor los/las peores
ugly	feo	*uglier*	más feo	*ugliest*	el más feo etc
intelligent	inteligente	*more intelligent*	más inteligente	*most intelligent*	el más inteligente etc.
useful	útil	*more useful*	más útil	*most useful*	el más útil etc.

Verbs

Infinitives and present tense

Verbs are words which describe actions, including abstract states or changes. Most verb forms tell you who is doing the action and when it is done, as well as what is being done (the **www** address of the verb!). Whilst in English the **who** idea is expressed mostly by a person word (I, you, he, she, it, we, they) in front of the verb, in Spanish the verb ending is enough to show this, and person words (subject pronouns) are only used when clarification or emphasis is needed. The subject pronouns are included in the tables below just for clarity. The verb endings also show **when** the action is done – past, present or future. Here are examples, of the three main types of Spanish verb in the **present** tense. The headings of the tables show the **infinitive** of the verb, the part of the verb without the person ending, and the form found in dictionaries and wordlists meaning '*to* ...'.

pronoun	**hablar** (infinitive)	*to speak*
yo	hablo	*I speak*
tú*	hablas	*you speak* (familiar)
él / ella /	habla	*he / she speaks,*
usted*		*you speak* (formal)
nosotros/as	hablamos	*we speak*
vosotros/as*	habláis	*you speak* (familiar plural)
ellos / ellas /	hablan	*they speak*
ustedes*		*you speak* (formal plural)

pronoun	**comer** (infinitive)	*to eat*
yo	como	*I eat*
tú*	comes	*you eat* (familiar)
él / ella /	come	*he / she eats,*
usted*		*you eat* (formal)
nosotros/as	comemos	*we eat*
vosotros/as*	coméis	*you eat* (familiar plural)
ellos / ellas /	comen	*they eat*
ustedes*		*you eat* (formal plural)

pronoun	**vivir** (infinitive)	*to live*
yo	vivo	*I live*
tú*	vives	*you live* (familiar)
él / ella /	vive	*he / she lives,*
usted*		*you live* (formal)
nosotros/as	vivimos	*we live*
vosotros/as*	vivís	*you live* (familiar plural)
ellos / ellas /	viven	*they live*
ustedes*		*you live* (formal plural)

* **usted** and **ustedes** are the 'formal' or 'polite' ways of saying *you*, singular and plural. For historical reasons, they are used with the he/she/it form of the verb. The 'informal' or 'familiar' words for *you* are **tú** and **vosotros/as** (the latter has masculine and feminine forms). In most cases, strangers will address you as **usted**, though when speaking to friends and younger people, **tú** is used. If in doubt, use **usted** until and unless invited to use **tú**. A Spanish person may invite you to use **tú** by saying **Podemos tutearnos, ¿no?**

Throughout this book when verb forms are translated, *you* is translated as either **tú** or **usted**, depending on which is most likely for the expression translated; sometimes both are given, but if you see *, it is to remind you that you need to decide on which to use. The object pronoun for **tú** is **te**, and for **usted** is **le**. Both are usually given, for you to choose.

The *I* form is known as the first person singular, *you* as the second person singular, *he / she / it* as the third person singular, *we* as the first person plural, *you* (plural) as the second person plural, and *they* as the third person plural.

It is useful to learn these verb patterns by heart, so that using them, and choosing the correct one becomes automatic.

Here are the patterns for some other useful verbs in the present tense:

ser*	*to be*	soy, eres, es, somos, sois, son
estar*	*to be*	estoy, estás, está, estamos, estáis, están
tener	*to have*	tengo, tienes, tiene, tenemos, tenéis, tienen
ir	*to go*	voy, vas, va, vamos, vais, van
hacer	*to do*	hago, haces, hace, hacemos, hacéis, hacen

*There are two verbs for *to be* in Spanish: *ser* is used for *permanent* notions, often describing the *essence* of something or somebody; *estar* is used to describe *where* somebody or something is, or what *state* they are in.

Here are the infinitives and first person (*I* form) of 26 of the most useful verbs. In the majority of cases you can probably work out the other forms for yourself, but because some are less predictable (irregular) it is worth checking them in a good dictionary, grammar book or verb book:

to answer	contestar; contesto
to arrive	llegar; llego
to ask	preguntar; pregunto
to be able to	poder; puedo
to bring / fetch	traer; traigo
to call (phone)	llamar; llamo
to cancel	anular; anulo
to find	encontrar; encuentro
to forget	olvidar; olvido
to give	dar; doy
to go in	entrar; entro
to go out	salir; salgo
to have to	tener que...; tengo que...
to know (a person, place)	conocer; conozco
to know (a fact, how to...)	saber; sé

to leave	irse; me voy
to look for	buscar; busco
to need	necesitar; necesito
to put	poner; pongo
to regret	lamentar; lamento
to remember	recordar; recuerdo
to reserve / book	reservar; reservo
to see	ver; veo
to take	tomar; tomo / coger; cojo
to want	querer; quiero
to write	escribir; escribo

Note how the *I* form always ends in -o, except **soy**, **estoy**, **voy** and **doy**. As you come to learn more verbs forms, you will find more patterns like this.

Reflexive verbs

Some verbs have a special 'person word' in front of them where the action described in some way 'bounces back', affecting the person doing the action. In English, these are called reflexive verbs and have a 'self' word attached, i.e. *I wash myself*.

Here is a typical reflexive verb set out in full; remember that the subject pronoun in the first column is not usually needed but the reflexive pronoun (in the second column) is always used:

subject pronoun	reflexive pronoun	lavarse (infinitive)	*to wash oneself*
yo	me	lavo	*I wash myself*
tú	te	lavas	*you wash yourself* (familiar)
él/ella/ usted	se	lava	*he / she washes himself / herself, you wash yourself* (formal)
nosotros/as	nos	lavamos	*we wash ourselves*
vosotros/as	vos	laváis	*you wash yourselves* (familiar plural)
ellos/ellas/ ustedes	se	lavan	*they wash themselves you wash yourselves* (formal plural)

Here are some more useful reflexive verbs. Notice the **se** attached to the end of the infinitive – this reminds you that the verb is reflexive. You will also recognize that many reflexive verbs describe everyday routine actions we do to ourselves. The first person form of each verbs is also given to you.

to wake up	despertarse	me despierto	*I wake up*
to get up	levantarse	me levanto	*I get up*
to wash oneself	lavarse	me lavo	*I wash myself*
to have a shower	ducharse	me ducho	*I have a shower*
to dress oneself	vestirse	me visto	*I get dressed*
to have a shave	afeitarse	me afeito	*I have a shave*
to comb one's hair	peinarse	me peino	*I comb my hair*
to put on make-up	maquillarse	me maquillo	*I put on make-up*
to have a bath	bañarse	me baño	*I have a bath*
to go to bed	acostarse	me acuesto	*I go to bed*
to go to sleep	dormirse	me duermo	*I go to sleep*
to go for a walk	pasearse	me paseo	*I go for a walk*
to be called	llamarse	me llamo	*I am called*
to leave / go away	irse	me voy	*I'm going / leaving*
to fall (down)	caerse	me caigo	*I fall down*

NB The reflexive form of some other verbs is used to express the idea of, for example, two people seeing each other: nos vemos todos los días – we see each other every day.

Talking about the past

Verbs have past tense forms to indicate actions which have already been done. With the exception of the perfect tense, the past tenses are formed by adding an ending to the stem of infinitive. Here are some examples with **hablar** – *to speak*:

tense	use	example	endings
preterite	single completed actions	*I spoke*	hablé, hablaste, habló, hablamos, hablasteis, hablaron
imperfect	ongoing, repeated action	*I was speaking*	hablaba, hablabas, hablaba, hablábamos, hablabais, hablaban
perfect	single, completed recent actions	*I have spoken*	he hablado, has hablado, ha hablado, hemos hablado, habéis hablado, han hablado

Note that each tense has some very definite distinguishing feature, the **sign** of that tense, either in its shape (perfect: two words), in its spelling (imperfect: -ab- or -í-) or its stress pattern (the preterite mostly has stress on the first syllable of its endings). The perfect tense is very straightforward in Spanish: the present tense of the verb **haber** is used for the first part of it, together with the past participle of the main verb.

As you can see, for single, completed actions at a specific time in the past, you can use the perfect tense if the action was recent, or the preterite if not recent. You use the imperfect tense when you are talking about something that was happening, or used to happen, or for descriptions in the past.

Here are ten useful verbs in the preterite:

infinitive	meaning	forms	meaning
ir / ser	*to go / to be*	fui, fuiste, fue, fuimos, fuisteis, fueron	*I went* etc.
venir	*to come*	vine, viniste, vino, vinimos, vinisteis, vinieron	*I came* etc.
entrar	*to go in, to enter*	entré, entraste, entró, entramos, entrasteis, entraron	*I entered* etc.
salir	*to go out*	salí, saliste, salió, salimos, salisteis, salieron	*I went out* etc.
despertarse	*to wake up*	me desperté, te despertaste, se despertó, nos despertamos, os despertasteis, se despertaron	*I woke up* etc.
tomar	*to take* (also *to eat/drink*)	tomé, tomaste, tomó, tomamos, tomasteis, tomaron	*I took* etc.
levantarse	*to get up*	me levanté, te levantaste, se levantó, nos levantamos, os levantasteis, se levantaron	*I got up* etc.
comer	*to eat*	comí, comiste, comió, comimos, comisteis, comieron	*I ate* etc.
beber	*to drink*	bebí, bebiste, bebió, bebimos, bebisteis, bebieron	*I drank* etc.
divertirse	*to enjoy yourself*	me divertí, te divertiste, se divirtió, nos divertimos, os divertisites, se divirtieron	*I enjoyed myself* etc.

Here are 15 useful verbs in the imperfect tense. Only the first three are given in full, since, once you have the first person (I) form, the remaining forms of the rest follow predictably, with the exception of **ser** and **ir**.

I was	era, eras, era, éramos, éramos, erais, eran
I was going	iba, ibas, iba, íbamos, ibais, iban
I had	tenía, tenías, tenía, teníamos, teníais, tenían
I could	podía
I was drinking	bebía
I was working	trabajaba
I was studying	estudiaba
I was eating	comía
I was talking	hablaba
I was travelling	viajaba
I used to live	vivía
I used to visit	visitaba
I used to see	veía
I used to want	quería
I used to know	sabía

Talking about the future

The future tense is always formed by adding the appropriate endings to the infinitive or an adopted form of it. Therefore, its distinguishing feature is always an -r- before the appropriate ending. The endings are the same for all verbs, without exception.

hablaré, hablarás, hablará, hablaremos, hablaréis, hablarán

The endings after *hablar* are the same for all verbs, with no exceptions.

There is another way of talking about future events if they are on the point of happening. As in English, you can use the present tense of **ir** (*to go*) with *a* and the infinitive of the main verb:

I am going to sing	voy a cantar
you are going to listen	vas a escuchar
he is going to play	va a jugar
we are going to watch	vamos a mirar
you (pl.) *are going to go out*	vais a salir
they are going to finish	van a terminar

Here are some of the most commonly used verbs in the future tense; note that some have slight spelling changes to the infinitive, though the endings are all the same as those shown previously. Only the first person form is given – you can work out the others.

to go	ir	*I will go*	iré
to arrive	llegar	*I will arrive*	llegaré
to know	saber	*I will know*	sabré
to want	querer	*I will want*	querré
to go out	salir	*I will go out*	saldré
to put	poner	*I will put*	pondré
to have	tener	*I will have*	tendré
to come	venir	*I will come*	vendré
to say	decir	*I will say*	diré
to do	hacer	*I will do*	haré

Here are some useful phrases in the future tense:

I will go – will you be going to the meeting?	Iré yo; ¿vas a ir a la reunión?
I will be OK. Will you be all right?	Estaré bien. Y tú, ¿vas a estar bien?
I will do it. Will you do it?	Voy a hacerlo. ¿Lo harás tú?
Will you take the bus?	¿Vas a coger el autobús?
How will you go?	¿Cómo vas a ir?
When will you arrive?	¿A qué hora llegarás?
When will you leave?	¿Cuándo te irás?
What will the weather be like?	¿Qué tiempo hará?
How much will it cost?	¿Cuánto costará?
Will it be suitable for children?	¿Será adecuado para los niños?
What will he do?	¿Qué hará él?
What will he have to drink?	Él, ¿qué va a tomar?
What will you take?	¿Qué vas a llevar?
When will it be?	¿Cuándo será?
Is it going to rain? Or will it snow?	¿Lloverá, o va a nevar?
Will it be fine?	¿Hará buen tiempo?
Will there be much traffic?	¿Habrá mucho tráfico?
There will be a lot of work.	Habrá mucho trabajo.

Conditional and subjunctives

Special verb forms are used for expressing conditions, wishes and so on. Here are examples of these:

me **gustaría**   I would like
no quiero que **vayas**   I don't wish you to go

The first of these is a good example of the conditional. You may have spotted that, as with the future, the ending is put after the whole of the infinitive. Therefore all forms have an -r- in them. You may also recognise the ending – the same as the imperfect endings for –er and –ir verbs. Here are some useful expressions, using all forms of the conditional:

to prefer	preferir	Preferiría ir al bar.
		I would prefer to go to the bar.
to feel like	apetecer	¿Te apetecería un café?
		Do you feel like a coffee?
to like	gustar	¿Le gustaría un aperitivo?
		Would you like an aperitif?
to appreciate	apreciar	El apreciaría tu ayuda.
		He would appreciate your help.
to be able to	poder	Ella podría ir mañana.
		She could go tomorrow.
to go	ir	Iríamos si pudiéramos.
		We would go if we could.
to have	tener	¿Tendríais tiempo?
		Would you have time?
to be	ser	Ustedes serían bienvenidos.
		You would be welcome.
to do	hacer	Ellos lo harían mañana.
		They would do it tomorrow.
to take	coger	Ellas cogerían el primer tren.
		They would catch the first train.

The subjunctive is a special verb form used where there is doubt or uncertainty, and in some command forms, and it has its own forms and endings. Here are some useful expressions using the subjunctive:

¡No hagas eso!	*Don't do that!*
¡No me mires así!	*Don't look at me like that!*
¡Hable despacio, por favor!	*Speak slowly, please!*
Deme un kilo de azúcar, por favor.	*Give me a kilo of sugar, please.*
Dígame, ¿dónde está Correos?	*Tell me, where is the post office?*
Te digo que no salgas.	*I'm telling you not to go out.*
Quiero que cierres la puerta.	*I want you to close the door.*
Nos dicen que no vayamos.	*They are telling us not to go.*
Le dijeron que no entrara.	*They told him not to go in.*
No queríais que él fuera a España.	*You didn't want him to go to Spain.*

Negative expressions – saying you don't!

The Spanish word **no** means both *no* and *not,* and it is often used by itself. Other negative expressions are given below, and **no** is used in front of the verb to introduce a negative. Negative expressions can also be used by themselves in front of the verb. Here are some useful negative expressions:

No como carne, no me gusta.	*I don't eat meat, I don't like it.*
No, no quiero salir.	*No, I don't want to go out.*
No tiene nada.	*He has nothing. /*
	He hasn't got anything.
No vale nada.	*Nothing is any good.*
No vio a nadie.	*She saw nobody.*
Nadie va a aquella tienda.	*No one goes to that shop.*
No trabajamos nunca en casa.	*We never work at home.*
Jamás voy en autobús.	*I never go by bus.*
No rompí ninguna ventana.	*I broke no windows.*
No tiene ni familia ni amigos.	*He has neither family nor friends.*

Here are some further useful examples of negative expressions.

My friend doesn't have a car.	Mi amigo no tiene coche.
I don't have a bike.	No tengo bicicleta.
I don't watch TV.	No veo la tele.
I don't smoke.	No fumo.
I don't go there any more.	Ya no voy allí.
I won't see him / her any more.	Ya no lo / la veré más.
I don't play any more.	Ya no juego.
Didn't you book a table?	¿No reservaste una mesa?
No they didn't answer the phone.	No, no contestaron el teléfono.
Didn't you get to the bank?	¿No llegaste al banco?
No, it wasn't open.	No, no estaba abierto.
Didn't you speak to him?	¿No hablaste con él?
Didn't you get tickets for the match?	¿No conseguiste entradas para el partido?
No, there weren't any left.	No quedaban.
Didn't you see your friend?	¿No viste a tu amigo?
No, he wasn't in.	No estaba.
Don't walk on the grass.	No pisar la hierba.
No entry	Prohibido entrar
No exit	Prohibido salir por aquí
No admission	No hay acceso
No smoking	No fumar
No dogs	Prohibido el acceso a perros

Don't do it!	¡No lo haga(s)!
Don't eat it!	¡No lo coma(s)!
Don't open the window.	No abra(s) la ventana.
Don't cross the road.	Prohibido cruzar la carretera.
... is not allowed / permitted	no se permite ...

Interrogative – asking questions

In English we sometimes ask questions by reversing the subject (person) and verb, so that, for example, the statement 'He is in a meeting' becomes 'Is he in a meeting?' as a question. In Spanish this is not practical, because the subject pronoun is not usually used. In spoken Spanish, the rise and fall of the voice (intonation) shows whether a question or a statement is intended – the voice rises at the end of a question, falls at the end of a statement. As a result, an ordinary sentence and a question can have the same words in the same order. In written Spanish an upside-down question mark shows a question is on the way. Thus:

¿Hablas inglés?	*Do you speak English?*
Hablas inglés.	*You speak English.*
Te gustan las manzanas.	*You like apples.*
¿Te gustan las manzanas?	*Do you like apples?*

Here are some more examples of questions; the normal answer expected would begin with **sí** or **no**:

Did you go to town?	¿Fuiste a la ciudad?
Have you seen him?	¿Le viste?
Did you try the steak?	¿Probaste el bistec?
Have you seen the film?	¿Has visto la película?
Do you drive a car?	¿Conduces un coche?
Do you smoke?	¿Usted fuma?
Do you prefer red or white wine?	¿Prefiere usted vino tinto o blanco?
Do you eat fish?	¿Comes pescado?
Are you taking medication?	¿Está tomando medicina / medicamento?

There are several words which can introduce a question, as you can see in the following examples:

| **¿Quién** abrió la puerta? | **Who** *opened the door?* |
| **¿Qué** tienes en la mano? | **What** *have you got in your hand?* |

¿**Por qué** haces eso?	*Why are you doing that?*
¿**Para qué** lo quieres?	*What do you want it for?*
¿**Dónde** está tu amiga?	*Where is your girlfriend?*
¿**Cuál** quieres?	*Which one do you want?*
¿**Cuáles** quieres?	*Which ones do you want?*
¿**Cuándo** va a llegar el tren?	*When will the train arrive?*
¿**Cuánto** dinero necesitas?	*How much money do you need?*
¿**Cuántas** manzanas quieres?	*How many apples do you want?*
¿**Durante cuánto** tiempo estás allí?	*How long are you there for?*

Remember that you need to consider whether you are addressing the other person formally (**usted**) or informally (**tú**), as this will affect the form of the verb.

Adverbs

You will remember that adjectives add information about nouns. In the same way, the main use of adverbs is to add information about actions. Many useful adverbs are based on adjectives: just as in English we add –*ly* to the adjective, Spanish adds –**mente** to the feminine form (if there is one – otherwise use the masculine). There are a few adverbs which don't follow this pattern – you will just have to learn these separately. The following table shows some useful adverbs (both regular and irregular in the way they are formed).

adjective	adjective	adverb	adverb
		muy	*very*
		bastante	*quite*
mucho	*much*	más	*more, most*
poco	*little*	menos	*less, fewer*
bueno	*good*	bien	*well*
bueno	*good*	mejor	*better, best*
malo	*bad*	peor	*worse, worst*
malo	*bad*	mal	*badly*
rápido	*quick, fast, rapid*	rápidamente	*quickly, fast, rapidly*
lento	*slow*	lentamente	*slowly*
inmediato	*immediate*	inmediatamente	*immediately*
completo	*complete*	completamente	*completely*
repentino	*sudden*	de repente, repentino	*suddenly*

silencioso	*noiseless*	silenciosamente	*noiselessly*
doloroso	*painful*	dolorosamente	*painfully*
feliz	happy	felizmente	*happily*
condescend- iente	*condescend- ing*	con condescencia	*condescend- ingly*
apropiado	*appropriate*	apropiadamente	*appropriately*
económico	*economic*	económicamente	*economically*
técnico	*technical*	técnicamente	*technically*
triste	*sad*	tristemente	*sadly*
frecuente	*frequent*	frecuentemente	*frequently*
previo	*previous*	previamente	*previously*
temprano	*early*	más temprano	*earlier*
próximo	*next*	próximamente	*next*

Here are some additional adverbs and adverbial phrases, which do not fit into any pattern.

pocas veces	*rarely*
de vez en cuando	*occasionally*
a veces	*sometimes*
a menudo	*often*
muy a menudo	*very often*
ahora	*now*
ya	*already*
pronto	*soon*
antes	*before*
después	*afterwards*
entonces, luego	*then*
temprano	*early*
tarde	*late*
más tarde	*later*
un poco	*a little*

Just like adjectives, adverbs can also have comparative and superlative forms. They are formed in the same way, as shown in the first two examples in the following table; note also the special forms based on **bien** and **mal**:

adverb	comparative	superlative	adverb	comparative	superlative
rápida- mente	más rápida- mente	lo más rápidamente	*fast*	*faster*	*fastest*
lenta- mente	más lenta- mente	lo más lenta- mente	*slow*	*slower*	*slowest*
bien	mejor	lo mejor	*well*	*better*	*best*
mal	peor	lo peor	*badly*	*worse*	*worst*

Colours and sizes

Colours *los colores*

Here is a list of common colours. Remember, these are all adjectives, so they go after the noun and follow the usual rules of agreement with nouns. To remind you, those ending in –o can also have the endings –a (fem), -os (masc. plural) and –as (fem. plural); those ending in any other vowel or a consonant just have a plural ending in –es. There are also three which are invariable, marked (inv.), which don't change at all.

black	negro
blue	azul
brown	marrón
green	verde
grey	gris
mauve	malva (inv.)
orange	naranja (inv.)
pink	rosa (inv.)
purple	purpúreo
red	rojo
white	blanco
yellow	amarillo

Here are examples of colours in use:

a red car	un coche rojo
a black suit	un traje negro
a pink jumper	un jersey rosa
a pink blouse	una blusa rosa
a blue shirt	una camisa azul
blue trainers	zapatillas azules
grey shoes	zapatos grises
brown gloves	guantes marrones

Finally, here is a list of most of the other colours you are likely to need.

cream / ivory	color crema	*emerald*	verde esmeralda
scarlet	(color) escarlata	*olive green*	verde oliva
		dark green	verde claro
lilac	(color) lila	*ruby*	(color) rubí
light/pale blue	azul claro	*salmon pink*	color salmón
navy blue	azul marino	*fuchsia*	fucsia
royal blue	azul real	*burgundy*	granate
dark blue	azul oscuro	*bright red*	rojo fuerte / vivo
turquoise	azul turquesa	*blue-grey*	gris azulado

sapphire	azul zafiro	*bottle green*	verde botella
khaki	caqui	*pale green*	verde claro
		beige	(color) beige

Sizes

Sizes too are adjectives, and follow the normal rules on position and agreement.

very small	muy pequeño, pequeñito, chico
small	pequeño
medium, average	mediano
large	grande
very large	muy grande
wide	ancho
narrow	estrecho
long	largo
short (people / stature)	bajo
short (objects)	corto

Numbers, times, days and dates

Cardinal numbers *los números cardinales*

1	uno / una	11	once	21	veintiuno/a
2	dos	12	doce	22	veintidós
3	tres	13	trece	23	veintitrés
4	cuatro	14	catorce	24	veinticuatro
5	cinco	15	quince	25	veinticinco
6	seis	16	dieciséis	26	veintiséis
7	siete	17	diecisiete	27	vientisiete
8	ocho	18	dieciocho	28	veintiocho
9	nueve	19	diecinueve	29	veintinueve
10	diez	20	veinte	30	treinta

31	treinta y uno / una etc
40	cuarenta etc
50	cincuenta
60	sesenta
70	setenta
80	ochenta
90	noventa
100	cien (*on its own and before nouns*); ciento (*before numbers*)

101	ciento uno	400	cuatrocientos
102	ciento dos	500	quinientos

110	ciento diez	1,000	mil
150	ciento cincuenta	2,000	dos mil
200	doscientos/as	2,100	dos mil diez
300	trescientos	5,000	cinco mil
		10,000	diez mil

million un millón
billion   un billón (*also* mil millones)

- Numbers written as figures just as in English, except that 7 is always crossed 7̶.
- When saying a long number aloud, such as a telephone number, Spanish people either say each number individually or they split the numbers into pairs (note that if there is an odd number, the first three may be expressed as hundreds):

   9865423 = nueve-ocho-seis-cinco-cuatro-dos-tres
   or   novecientos ochenta y seis, cincuenta y cuatro, veintitrés

- In Spanish, as in most other European countries, a full stop is used to indicate thousands instead of a comma, and a comma is used where we use a decimal point.

   tres mil doscientos quince = 3.215
   dieciséis coma cuatro = 16,4

Ordinal numbers *los números ordinales*

These are adjectives ... so remember the rules!

first	primero	*fifth*	quinto
second	segundo	*tenth*	décimo
third	tercero	*21st*	veintiún (e.g. *21st*
fourth	cuarto		*birthday* el veintiún cumpleaños)

Here are some fractions:

half	la mitad	*quarter*	el cuarto
third	el tercio	*fifth*	el quinto

dates *fechas*

the century	el siglo
the nineteen hundreds	el siglo diecinueve
the 20th century	el siglo veinte
the 21st century	el siglo veintiuno

the 22nd century	el siglo veintidós
the millennium	el milenio
the 1990s	los años noventa
the year 2000	el año dos mil
the year 2010	el año dos mil diez
next year	el año próximo, el año que viene (*counted from now*)
last year	el año pasado
the year before last	el año antepasado
the year after next	el año que viene no, el siguiente

Days and months *días y meses*

In Spanish days of the week and months of the year are written with a small letter, (except for when they start a sentence). They are all masculine.

Monday	lunes	*Saturday*	sábado
Tuesday	martes	*Sunday*	domingo
Wednesday	miércoles	*on Thursday*	el jueves
Thursday	jueves	*on Saturdays*	los sábados
Friday	viernes		
January	enero	*July*	julio
February	febrero	*August*	agosto
March	marzo	*September*	septiembre
April	abril	*October*	octubre
May	mayo	*November*	noviembre
June	junio	*December*	diciembre

Expressions of time

day	el día
week	la semana
month	el mes
year	el año
last year / month	el año / mes pasado
last week	la semana pasada
next week	la semana que viene
next month / year	el mes / el año que viene
yesterday	ayer
the day before yesterday	anteayer
today	hoy

tomorrow	mañana
the day after tomorrow	pasado mañana
early morning	la madrugada
morning	la mañana
afternoon	la tarde
evening	la tarde
night	la noche
tomorrow morning	mañana por la mañana
yesterday afternoon	ayer (por la) tarde
this afternoon	esta tarde
tonight	esta noche

The seasons *las estaciones*

spring	la primavera	*autumn*	el otoño
summer	el verano	*winter*	el invierno

The clock *el reloj*

What time is it?	¿Qué hora es?
midday / midnight	es mediodía / medianoche
1 o'clock	es la una
2 o'clock	son las dos
3.05	son las tres y cinco
4.10	son las cuatro y diez
5.15	son las cinco y cuarto
6.20	son las seis y veinte
7.25	son las siete y veinticinco
8.30	son las ocho y media
9.35	son las diez menos veinticinco
10.40	son las once menos veinte
11.45	son las doce menos cuarto
12.50	es la una menos diez
13.55	son las dos menos cinco

You can see that Spanish uses **es ...** before 1 o'clock, midday and midnight, which is quite logical since all are singular, then **son las...** for the rest, which are plural. You will also by now have worked out that from the hour to half past, you simply add **y** and the number, **cuarto** or **med**ia, and then use **menos** from half past up to the hour, calculating backwards from the next hour as in English. You can also add **de la madrugada, de la mañana, de la tarde** and **de la noche** to be precise, such as in the example:

It is four o'clock in the afternoon. Son las cuatro de la tarde.

The 24-hour clock is also used very widely in Spain, especially on the radio and for transport. In these instances the times are expressed pretty much as in English:

It is 0900 hours.	Son las cero nueve horas.
It is 1315.	Son las trece quince (horas).
It is 2245.	Son las veintidós cuarenta y cinco.

Finally, some extra vocabulary and expressions to do with time:

second	el segundo	*hour*	la hora
minute	el minuto	*half hour*	la media hora
clock, watch	el reloj	*alarm clock*	el despertador
What time is it?		¿Qué hora es?	
Have you got the time?		¿Tiene hora?	

early	temprano
late	tarde
sooner or later	tarde o temprano
Better late than never!	¡Más vale tarde que nunca!
sunset	la puesta del sol
sunrise	la salida del sol
dawn / daybreak	el alba (f)/ el amanecer
dusk / nightfall	el anochecer
telling the time	decir la hora
My watch has stopped.	No anda mi reloj. / Mi reloj no funciona.
… is (… minutes) fast / slow	va (… minutos) adelantado / atrasado

Quantity

weight	el peso	*length*	la longitud
height	la altura / la estatura	*size*	la talla (*clothes*), el número (*shoes*)

Weights and measures *los pesos y las medidas*

kilo	el kilo
half a kilo	el medio kilo
500 grams	quinientos gramos / medio kilo
a pound	una libra

a litre	un litro	a kilometre	un kilómetro
a metre	un metro	a pair	un par
a centimetre	un centímetro	a dozen	una docena

bottle	una botella	box	una caja
jar	un bote	pot	un pote / tarro
tin	una lata	package	un paquete

lots of (e.g. sugar)	mucho (azúcar)
lots of (e.g. meat)	mucha (carne)
lots of (e.g. lemons)	muchos (limones)
lots of (e.g. apples)	muchas (manzanas)
a little ...	un poco de ...
a few ...	unos cuantos/as ...
more of	más ...

a portion of	una ración de	about 20	una veintena
about 10	una decena	about 100	un centenar
about 15	una quincena	about 1,000	un millar

Exclamations, giving orders and being polite

How to say *please* and *thank you!*

Thank you	¡Gracias!
Please	Por favor

Bear in mind that Spanish people don't use *please* or *thank you* quite as often with close family and friends, where relationships tend to be 'warmer', and they are deemed not to be as essential. Therefore, if a Spaniard says to you in English *Give me the salt!*, he is not being impolite or unfriendly – he is simply expressing himself the way he would in Spanish. You could even assume it is showing that he considers you close enough not to need a formula of politeness, the 'lubricating oil' of relationships!

However, you will find that Spanish people say far more often than we do: ¡de nada!, or ¡no hay de que! when you say *thank you* – two ways of saying *don't mention it*.

Giving orders / commands

You will remember that Spanish has four ways of saying *you*: familiar singular (**tú**), polite singular (**usted**), familiar plural (**vosotros/as**) and polite plural (**ustedes**). Look back to p. 16 to remind yourself when to use each form. In general, when giving orders to strangers you need to use the formal or polite forms.

Help!	¡Socorro!
Fire!	¡Fuego!
Cheers! (with drink)	¡Salud!
Cheers! (thanks)	¡Gracias!
Cheers (goodbye)	¡Chao!
Cheerio	¡Chao!
Please	Por favor
Wait!	¡Espere!
Stop!	¡Pare!
Listen!	¡Escuche!
Look!	¡Mire!
Pass me a knife.	Deme un cuchillo.
Fetch a glass.	Traiga / tráigame un vaso.
Take the chocolates.	Tome los chocolates.
Bring me my bag.	Tráigame mi bolso.
Excuse me (listen to me).	Oiga. / Oigame. / Por favor.
Excuse me (sorry).	Perdone / Perdón.
Excuse me (I want to pass).	Con permiso.
I'm sorry.	Lo siento.
I didn't mean it.	Fue sin querer.
I didn't know.	No lo sabía.
I didn't understand.	No (le) comprendí(a) / entendí(a).
Sorry I'm late	Siento llegar tarde / con retraso.

Being polite

yes, please	sí, por favor
no, thank you	no, gracias
don't mention it	de nada
not at all	no hay de qué
Pardon? (please repeat)	¿cómo?
I didn't catch what you said.	No le oí bien.
I don't understand.	No entiendo / comprendo.
Can I help you?	¿En qué puedo ayudarle?
Can you help me?	¿Me puede ayudar?
Can you say it again?	Repita, por favor.
Can you speak more slowly please?	Hable más despacio, por favor.
Please will you write it down?	Por favor, escríbalo.

Spanish spelling quirks

This section offers tips to help you cope with the 'spelling quirks' of Spanish, and the peculiarities of Spanish punctuation. First a few odd points:

- Many English words containing a double consonant (such as *accent*) have a single consonant in Spanish (**acento**).
- Spanish accents do not alter the sound of the letter that carries one, but the syllable in which it occurs is pronounced more loudly than the rest of the word (see p. 9). This can be crucial in verb forms, such as: **hablo** *I speak*; **habló** *he / she / you spoke*.
- As you have seen on p. 31, Spanish uses capital letters less than English, notably not on names of days and months, nationalities and names of languages.
- Punctuation is mostly the same as in English, except for the use of upside-down question marks and exclamation marks at the beginning of a question or exclamation. This serves to show that a question or exclamation follows, so that if you are reading aloud you can adjust your intonation accordingly. In a question the voice rises towards the end, whilst in a normal statement, it rises before a comma, but falls at a colon, semi-colon or full stop. In an exclamation, the most important words are spoken with more emphasis.

If you are aware of the following 'spelling quirks' you will be able to work out the meaning of many more Spanish words. The meaning of some of the Spanish words are given, but where the meaning is not given it is because it should be obvious!

'Vowel stretching' of *e* and *o*

When these two letters are stressed, they often change and 'stretch' in the Spanish version of a similar word in English:

---

e → **ie**, and *o* → **ue**; and sometimes *e* → **i**, *o* → **u** and *u* → **ue**

e → **ie**: b**ie**n = *well*; compare with Latin / Italian b**e**ne, English b**e**neficial

o → **ue**: b**ue**no = *good*; compare with French b**o**n, English b**o**nus

e → **i**: p**i**do = *I ask for*, from p**e**dir; compare with p**e**tition

o → **u**: d**u**rmió = *he slept*, from d**o**rmir; compare with d**o**rmitory

u → **ue**: ag**üe**ro = *augur*

Some of these can also work the other way round:

    pr**e**cio = *price*; d**e**scuento = *discount*

esc-, esp-, est-

Many words in English and French which begin with *sc-, sp-*
and *st-* begin in Spanish with **esc-, esp-, est-**. So, to guess at new
words with these beginnings, simply take off the e-. You'll be
surprised at how many new words you will now be able to
work out.

> **e** + **sc**: **esc**uela = *school*
> **e** + **sp**: **esp**añol = *Spanish*
> **e** + **st**: **est**udiante = *student*

Spanish replaces **y** in English with an **i**, and **-ía** or **-ia** at the end
of a word.

> **si**stema = *system*; **ri**tmo = *rhythm*; **sí**ntoma = *symptom*
> biolog**ía** = *biology*; farmac**ia** = *pharmacy*; Ital**ia** = *Italy*

Double consonants

Spanish has fewer double consonants than in English. However,
cc, **ll** and **rr** are all very common in Spanish; **nn** occurs in a few
words, usually those beginning with the prefix **in-**.

> ab**ad**ía (*abbey*), **ac**eptar, e**f**ecto, ba**l**ón, ma**m**ut, o**p**resor,
> pro**f**esor, psi**c**ología, melan**c**ólico, **c**aótico, **c**iencia, con**c**iencia
> N.B. **inn**ecesario – *unnecessary* (**in-** negating / opposite);
> **inn**ovar –= *to innovate* (**in-** meaning *into*)
>
> **cc** = **ct**: a**cc**ión, di**cc**ionario, ele**cc**ión

f/ph

Spanish does not have **ph** spellings, and uses **f** instead.

> atmós**f**era; **f**armacia; **f**ilosofía; geogra**f**ía; pro**f**eta; semá**f**oro

g/w

Spanish has problems with **w** sounds, especially at the beginning
of words; it tends to use **g** (**g** or **gu**) instead.

> **w** → **g**: (el País de) **G**ales = *Wales*; c.f. **G**alicia
> **gu**erra = *war*; c.f. *gu**errilla* / **gu**errillero
>
> *wh**isky* is often pronounced or written **gü**isky

j/x

Spanish usually uses **j** where English uses **x**.

> **x → j**: Méjico = *Mexico*; fijo = *fixed*

ll

Spanish often uses **ll** instead of **cl, fl,** and **pl** at the beginning of words.

> *cl* → **ll**: llamar = *to call*; c.f. ex*cl*aim (*call out*)
> *fl* → **ll**: llama = *flame*
> *pl* → **ll**: llano = *plain*

t/th

Spanish does not have **th** spellings and uses **t** instead.

> teología, terapia, teatro, ateo (*atheist*), simpatía

Tips on Spanish

Earlier (pp. 3–10) you were given some handy hints to help you learn – and more to the point – remember words. The 'spelling quirks' of Spanish have also been covered (see pp. 36–38) to help you to see connections which might otherwise be hidden. This section will give you some further hints to help you understand how words work in Spanish.

As we've already discussed there is a large overlap between Spanish and English vocabulary. This exists because about 60 per cent of English words come from Latin, and at least 90 per cent of Spanish words come from Latin: there is bound to be an overlap of words which both languages have taken from Latin – the so-called **cognates**! Apart from words which came into English from Norman French – words like *veal, beef, hostel* and *tailor,* – many Latin words were imported into English at a later stage to create terminology for newly defined aspects of art, literature and philosophy, such as *sculpture, epigram, ideology* and later science, such as *species, genus, geology,* and technology such as *astronaut, chronometer, spectroscope*.

In addition, English can be described as a 'layered' language: we often have two words for the same thing. There is often an everyday word of Anglo-Saxon origin, and a completely different 'Latinate' equivalent with a similar meaning, but used in more 'learned' or specialized language. 'Step up' in level of language from *speed* and you find a word meaning the same – *velocity* – which you probably would not use in everyday language. Since Spanish mostly comes directly from Latin, but with adapted spellings, the 'higher level' English words are often close to the everyday Spanish words, because Spanish does not have as many 'language layers'. For example:

a gran velocidad	*at great speed*
a toda velocidad	*at top speed*
velocidad económica	*cruising speed*
exceder la velocidad permitida	*to exceed the speed limit*
tercera velocidad	*third gear*

In a nutshell, the longer the English word is (i.e. the more specialized and 'learned') the more likely it is to be similar to the Spanish word! So, working from English to Spanish, think of a more 'upmarket' word with the same meaning, and the Spanish word you need will often be similar in spelling. Working from Spanish to English, try saying the word with an English accent, and you will sometimes find that you can understand it with no problem, but that the word you want in English will be the more downmarket synonym, the one with the same meaning used in everyday English.

Besides this there are, of course, lots of Spanish words we have 'borrowed', and lots of English words 'imported' into Spanish. The following list starts with these, which you will understand instantly, and moves on to types of word with less obvious connections, that need a bit more effort. The meanings of the Spanish words are only given if they are not obvious.

- English words imported into Spanish, with the same meaning
    e.g. álbum, récord, líder, fútbol, mánager.

- Words which English has borrowed from Spanish:
    e.g. paella, matador, fiesta, aficionado

- Words used in Spanish and English with the same spelling:
    e.g. hotel, panorama, taxi, normal

- Words similar in form to their English equivalent but with Spanish 'spelling quirks' as described above:
    e.g. documento, militar, sistema, clima, movimiento, millón

- Verbs whose basic part ('stem') is identical to or similar to English,

    e.g. admirar, contener, consistir, aplaudir, desarrollar
    (*to develop*, *unroll*)

- Words with common prefixes at the beginning and suffixes on the end; note the similarity between the English and Spanish in this list of the most common prefixes and suffixes:

a- = *a-/ab-*	e.g. **amoral** (*amoral*); **anormal** (*abnormal*)
con- = *con-*	e.g. **considerar** (to *consider*); **concierto** (*concert*)
des-/dis- = *dis-*	e.g. **desventaja** (*disadvantage*); **distinguir** (*to distinguish*)
il- = *il-*	e.g. **ilegal** (*illegal*); **ilógico** (*illogical*)
in- = *im-*	e.g. **inmediato** (*immediate*); **inmoderado** (*immoderate*)
in- = *in-*	e.g. **insuficiente** (*insufficient*); **inseparable** (*inseparable*)
in- = *un-*	e.g. **innecesario** (*unnecessary*); **ininteligible** (*unintelligible*)
ir- = *un-*	e.g. **irreal** (*unreal*); **irrepetible** (*unrepeatable*)
ir- = *ir-*	e.g. **irregular** (*irregular*); **irreducible** (*irreducible*)
re- = *re-*	e.g. **reinventar** (*reinvent*); **recuperar** (*to recuperate*)
sub- = *sub-*	e.g. **subsistir** – (*subsist*); **subdividir** (*subdivide*)
-able = *-able*	e.g. **probable** – (*probable*); **culpable** (*culpable*)
-ción = *-tion*	e.g. **acción** (*action*); **elección** (*election*)
-dad = *-ty*	e.g. **ciudad** (*city*); **capacidad** (*capacity*)
-ble = *-ible*	e.g. **imposible** (*impossible*); **susceptible** (*susceptible*)
-ía, -ia = *-y*	e.g. **energía** (*energy*); **farmacia** (*pharmacy*)
-ismo = *-ism*	e.g. **turismo** (*tourism*); **fascismo** (*fascism*)
-m(i)ento = *-ment*	e.g. **apartamento** (*apartment*); **desplazamiento** (*displacement*)

Once you have learnt a few Spanish words well, you will begin to realize that many words are built on other base words: if you know the base word, you can work out the meaning of the 'derived' form for yourself by 'undressing' the word to get back to the basics! You might have noticed this in the list above.

- Here are some clear examples of base words with their 'derivatives', whose meaning is adapted by common prefixes or suffixes added to the base word you already know:

  des-: hacer (*to do*) → **deshacer** (*to undo*)
  dis-: continuo (*continuous*) → **discontinuo** (*discontinuous*)
  in-/im-: correcto (*correct*) → **incorrecto** (*incorrect*)
    posible (*possible*) → **imposible** (*impossible*)
  re-: volver (*to [re]turn*) → **revolver** (*to revolve, turn round*)
  sub-: marino (*marine*) → **submarino** (*submarine*)
  -able-: salud (*health*) → **saludable** (*healthy*)
  miento-: pensar (*to think*) → **pensamiento** (*thought*)
  -oso: arena (*sand*) → **arenoso** (*sandy*)

- There are many nouns describing people, places of work and occupations based on, for example, the product involved or the verb describing what the person does. Here are some useful examples:

  zapato (*shoe*) → **zapatero, zapatería** (*shoemaker, shoe-shop*)
  pescado (*fish*) → **pescadero, pescadería** (*fishmonger, fish-shop*)
  pescar (*to fish*) → **pescador** (*fisherman*)
  jugar (*to play*) → **jugador** (*player*)
  pintar (*to paint*) → **pintor** (*painter*)
  piano (*piano*) → **pianista** (*pianist*)

- As explained earlier (see p. 26) most adverbs in Spanish are formed by adding the ending **-mente** to an adjective:

  e.g. **total** → **totalmente** (*total, totally*); **activo** → **activamente** (*active, actively*)

- A number of adjectives are formed with the ending **-able** or **-ible** added to the stem of a verb; many of them are almost the same as their English counterparts:

  e.g. **imaginar** → **imaginable**; **admirar** → **admirable**

- Other adjectives have the ending **-oso/-osa** added to a base noun; again, they are easily identifiable:

  e.g. **religión** → **religioso**; **furia** → **furioso**; **vicio** → **vicioso**

- Many adjectives of nationality or origin have the ending **-és/esa**, **-(i)ense**, **-eno/a**, **-eño/a** on the end of the basis of the name of the country or region:

  e.g. **Japón** → **japonés**; **Canadá** → **canadiense**; **Chile** → **chileno**, **Brasil** → **brasileño**

- You will easily recognize the diminutive forms ending in -**ito**, -**illo**, -**ico** derived from known words:

  e.g. **señorito, panecillo, casita, perrito**

- Similarly, there are augmentative (= bigger) and pejorative (= nasty) suffixes such as -**ón/ona**, -**azo**, -**ucho**:

  e.g. **hombrón** (*a big man*) **mujerona** (*big woman*); **manotazo** (*slap, smack – with the hand*); **casucha** (*hovel – horrible house!*)

- Spanish has many compound nouns, often consisting of combinations of verbs and nouns, in the order verb-noun, unlike English noun-verb!

  e.g. **abrelatas** (*bottle-opener*); **sacacorchos** (*cork-screw*); **cortacésped** (lawn-mower)

- There are many words derived from adjectives:

  e.g. **tranquilo** → **tranquilizar** (*to tranquilize*); **blanco** → **blanquear** (*to whiten*); **sucio** → **ensuciar** (*to dirty*); **limpio** → **limpieza** (*cleaning*)

- Equally, look out for words derived from verbs, with endings -**ante** or -**ente**:

  e.g. **cantar** → **cantante** (*singer*); **oír** → **oyente** (*listener*)

- Many place names are spelt in a similar way to the English equivalent:

  e.g. **Italia, América, Brasil, Argentina, Grecia, Londres, Cornualles, Edimburgo**

- Note that common acronyms and initials in Spanish may be in reverse order compared to English, following the different order of noun and adjective:

  e.g. UNO = **ONU – Organización de las Naciones Unidas**

  NATO = **OTAN – Organización del Tratado del Atlántico del Norte**

  Note also the abbreviation for the USA is **EEUU – los Estados Unidos**. Plural abbreviations double the initials used.

To persuade you how useful all this knowledge is, and just for fun, here is an alphabetical list of words with the commonest derivative ending, -**ción** or -**ión**, added to a base word. Most can also be considered cognates, since English has a version of most of them. The idea of this list is to prove a point and to give you confidence in your understanding of how Spanish words work ... but there are *hundreds* more, so see how many you can add to the lists!

A	adición, adicción, admiración, anticipación
B	bendición
C	condición, comprensión, continuación, creación
D	dedicación, dominación, definición
E	elevación, evaluación, estimación
F	fabricación, formación
G	generación, graduación
H	habitación
I	iniciación, introducción, invitación
J	jubilación, jerarquización
L	limitación, levitación
M	motivación
N	nominación
O	oposición, opinión
P	producción, participación
R	renovación, reunión, reservación, restauración
S	sensación, simplificación, situación
T	tentación, testificación
U	ubicación, utilización, usurpación
V	verificación, vacación
Y	yuxtaposición
Z	zonación

01

personal matters

1.1 Titles, greetings and making arrangements

Core vocabulary

titles	fórmulas de tratamiento
Mr	señor (Sr)
Mrs	señora (Sra)
Miss	señorita (Srta)
Sir / Mr	Don (D)
Madam / Mrs	Doña (Da)

- **Señor** is used for both *Mr* and *Sir*; the latter is used to a stranger by e.g. a shop assistant, and by a serviceman to a senior officer; **señora** is used for both *Mrs* and *Madam* in the same way, and **señorita** is always used for Miss. All of these are used with the person's surname, whether or not their first name is also being used, and are preceded with **el** or **la** except when you are speaking direct to him / her:

  el señor Juan Ribera; la señora Jiménez; '¡Hola, señorita López!'

- Spanish also has two other courtesy titles – **don / doña**: these are reserved for someone of some status or age, and must be used with the person's first name. You can also use them with **señor/a**, and the surname provided the first name is also used.

  el señor don Paco Peña; Señora doña Blanca López Román (*on a letter*); **'¡Buenos días, don José!'**

- Spanish people usually use **doctor** when referring to or addressing a doctor, even though the normal word for the profession is **médico**. A lawyer is referred to as **abogado**, and teachers can be addressed as **profesor**. The normal word for boss is **jefe**.

greetings	los saludos
Hello, hi	¡hola!
Good morning	buenos días
Good afternoon, Good evening	buenas tardes
Good night	buenas noches
Goodbye	adiós, chao (informal)

Note that **tarde** is used both for *afternoon* and *evening*, and lasts from lunchtime until dinner time, which is usually around 9 or 10 p.m. **Buenas noches** can be used when you meet up with someone late in the evening, as well as when you are leaving them to go home or to bed.

How to say *you*

Tutear / hablar de usted / tratar de usted

In Spanish, you need to decide how to address the person you are speaking to. The informal **tú** is used for family, close friends and acquaintances, and in most cases anyone of an age and status similar to yours, even if you don't yet know them. The formal **usted** is used for strangers and those older than you or senior in status. In Spain this is more relaxed than it used to be, but if in doubt when meeting someone for the first time, use **usted** until invited to use **tú**. Your new acquaintance will probably use an expression such as **podemos tutearnos** or **me puedes hablar de tú** to invite you to be informal.

introducing someone	*presentar a alguien*
This is ...	Éste / ésta es ...,
May I introduce ... ?	Te / le presento a ...
Are you (Mr ...)?	¿Es usted (el señor ...)?
Do you know (Mr ...)?	¿Conoce(s) a (Señor ...)?
Mr What's-his-name	el señor fulano
Mrs What's-her-name	la señora fulana
Pleased to meet you.	¡Encantado/a! / ¡Mucho gusto!

I am ...	*soy ...*
single	soltero/a
married	casado/a
divorced	divorciado/a
separated	separado/a
a widow	una viuda
a widower	un viudo

making plans	*hacer planes*
What shall we do this evening?	¿Qué vamos a hacer esta tarde?
May I invite you to a ...?	¿Puedo invitarte/le a ...?
bar	un bar
night club	un club nocturno
restaurant	un restaurante
theatre	(al) teatro
cinema	(al) cine
dance	un baile
drink	tomar algo
meal / lunch / dinner	comer / cenar
dance	bailar
show	un espectáculo
play	una obra de teatro

musical	un musical
comedy	una comedia
concert	un concierto
What would you like to do?	¿Qué te / le gustaría hacer?
Where would you like to go?	¿Adónde te / le gustaría ir?
When / where shall we meet?	¿Cuándo dónde nos vemos / quedamos?
I will pick you up.	Iré a buscarte/le.
to arrange a meeting	citarse
to book a table	reservar una mesa
to go to the cinema	ir al cine
to go to the theatre	ir al teatro
to go out	salir
to go to a night club	ir a un club nocturno
to watch a video	ver un vídeo

Useful phrases

How are you?	¿Cómo estás / está usted?
How's it going?	¿Qué tal?
Very well thank you.	Muy bien, gracias.
Have a nice day / weekend etc.	¡Que tengas un buen día / fin de semana!
May I sit here?	¿Puedo sentarme aquí?
Are you alone?	¿Está(s) solo/a?
See you soon.	Hasta pronto.
See you later.	Hasta luego.
See you next time.	Hasta la vista.
See you tomorrow.	Hasta mañana.
Excuse me	Discúlpame / discúlpeme
Pardon?	¿Cómo?
I don't understand	No entiendo / comprendo
Speak more slowly please	Habla / hable más despacio por favor
I apologize	Lo siento
I'm sorry	Lo siento
I beg your pardon	Perdóname / perdóneme
I didn't mean it	Lo hice sin querer
Forgive me	Perdóname / perdóneme
Sorry, it was my fault	Lo siento, fue culpa mía
It was your fault	Fue culpa tuya / suya
Thank you very much	Muchas gracias
I enjoyed it very much	Me gustó mucho
I had a lovely time	Lo pasé muy bien

We must do it again sometime	Deberíamos hacerlo otra vez
I will see you tomorrow / later	Te / le veré mañana / más tarde
I would like to see you again	Me gustaría verte/le otra vez
It's a pleasure	Es un placer
Have a good time!	¡Qué te diviertes / se divierta!
Have a safe journey	Buen viaje
Good luck	¡Mucha suerte!
All the best	¡Que tenga suerte!

Useful verbs

| to introduce | presentar, introducir |

1.2 Where are you from?

Core vocabulary

Where do you come from?	¿De dónde eres? / ¿De dónde es usted?
I come from ...	Soy de ...
I am ...	Soy ...
I speak ...	hablo ...

Austria	Austria	Austrian	austriaco/a
Belgium	Bélgica	Belgian	belga
Eire	Irlanda	Irish	irlandés, irlandesa
England	Inglaterra	English	inglés, inglesa
France	Francia	French	francés, francesa
Germany	Alemania	German	alemán, alemana
Greece	Grecia	Greek	griego/a
Italy	Italia	Italian	italiano/a
Scotland	Escocia	Scottish	escocés, escocesa
Spain	España	Spanish	español(a)
Switzerland	Suiza	Swiss	suizo/a
Wales	El País de Gales	Welsh	galés, galesa

In each case the masculine form of the nationality is the name of the language, except in the case of countries which do not have their own language.

Africa	África	African	africano/a
America	América	American	americano/a
Australia	Australia	Australian	australiano/a
Croatia	Croacia	Croatian	croata
Denmark	Dinamarca	Danish	danés, danesa

Finland	Finlandia	Finnish	finlandés, finlandesa
Hungary	Hungria	Hungarian	húngaro/a
India	India	Indian	indio/a
New Zealand	Nueva Zelanda/ Zelandia	New Zealander	neocelandés neocelandesa
Norway	Noruega	Norwegian	noruego/a
Poland	Polonia	Polish	polaco/a
Russia	Rusia	Russian	ruso/a
Sweden	Suecia	Swedish	sueco

Extras

There are a number of British geographical names for which there is a Spanish version:

the United Kingdom	el Reino Unido
Great Britain	Gran Bretaña
England	Inglaterra
Wales	el País de Gales
Scotland	Escocia
Northern Ireland	Irlanda del Norte
London	Londres
Edinburgh	Edimburgo
Thames	el Támesis
Cornwall	Cornualles

There are also a number of foreign cities which have a Spanish version:

Rome	Roma
Genoa	Génova
New York	Nueva York
Moscow	Moscú
Paris	París
Berlin	Berlín
Stockholm	Estocolmo
Hamburg	Hamburgo
the Hague	La Haya

Useful phrases

Do you speak English?	¿Hablas inglés? / ¿Habla usted inglés?
What languages do you speak?	¿Qué idiomas / lenguas habla(s)?
What nationality are you?	¿De qué nacionalidad eres / es usted?

Where were you born?	¿Dónde naciste / nació usted?
I was born in …	Nací en …
I live …	Vivo …
in the north / south /east / west	en el norte / sur / este / oeste
middle	en el centro
near the sea	cerca del mar
on the coast	en la costa
in the mountains	en las montañas
in the city	en la ciudad
in a village	en un pueblo / una aldea
in the suburbs	en los barrios
in the country	en el campo

Useful verbs

to live	vivir	*I live …*	vivo …
to speak	hablar	*I speak …*	hablo …
to be born	nacer	*I was born in …*	nací en …

1.3 Personal appearance

Core vocabulary

What are you like?	¿Cómo eres? / ¿Cómo es usted?
I am a …	Soy un(a) …
What does he / she …	¿Cómo …
He /she is a …	Es …
man	un hombre
woman	una mujer
girl	una chica
boy	un chico
teenager	un / una adolescente
child	un niño / una niña
baby	un bebé

Use the following grids to help you to build up what you need to be able to say to describe yourself and someone you know well:

I am Soy	*(quite* bastante)	*tall* alto/a	
Are you? ¿Eres? / ¿Es usted?	*(very* muy)	*small* pequeño/a *short* bajo/a	
He / She is Él / ella es ...		*average* mediano/a	

I have tengo *He has* (Él) tiene ... *She has* (Ella) tiene ...	*short / long hair* *medium-length hair* *blonde hair* *brown hair* *dark hair* *blue / brown eyes*	(el) pelo corto / largo (el) pelo mediano (el) pelo rubio (el) pelo castaño (el) pelo oscuro (los) ojos azules / marrón

attractive	atractivo/a	*unattractive*	no atractivo/a
fashionable	de moda	*unfashionable*	pasado de moda
fit	en buena forma	*unfit*	en mala forma
good looking	hermoso/a	*ugly*	feo/a
neat	aseado/a	*untidy*	descuidado
smart	elegante	*scruffy*	dejado
ordinary	ordinario	*different*	diferente
tall	alto/a	*short*	bajo/a
underweight	de peso insuficiente	*overweight*	gordo
well built	fornido/a	*weak/skinny*	flaco/a
anorexic	anoréxico/a	*obese*	obeso
right-handed	diestro	*left-handed*	zurdo
short-sighted	miope / corto de vista	*long-sighted*	présbita (inv)
agoraphobic	agorafóbico	*claustrophobic*	claustrofóbico

Here are some of the more colloquial words used in Spain to describe people:

butch (man)	macho
butch (woman)	marimacha
getting on a bit	de cierta edad
teenager	el adolescente
brat, kid, youngster	el mocoso/ crío
bird (girl)	la pollita

Useful phrases

How much do you weigh?	¿Cuánto pesas / pesa usted?
I weigh 75 kg	Peso 75 kg
How tall are you?	¿Cuánto mides / mide usted?
I am 1.59 m	Mido 1.59 m

Useful verbs

to look like someone	parecerse a alguien
to put on weight	engordar
to lose weight	adelgazar
to get fit	ponerse en forma

1.4 What sort of person are you?

Core vocabulary

character and feelings *carácter y sentimientos*

If you are describing somebody, you need to decide whether you are talking about their character, in which case you need an expression with the verb **ser**, or you are talking about how they are or how they feel, in which case you need an expression with the verb **estar** (see p. 17). Remember also that the adjectives have to agree with the noun.

I am	soy	*shy / talkative*	tímido / hablador
are you...?	¿eres / es usted...?	*happy / unhappy*	feliz / infeliz
he is	(él) es	*friendly / unfriendly*	amistoso / poco amistoso
she is	(ella) es (+ fem adj)	*nice / nasty*	simpático / antipático
I am	estoy	*happy / sad*	contento / triste
are you	¿estás / está usted?	*awake / tired*	despierto / cansado
he is	(él) está	*smart / scruffy*	guapo / mal vestido
she is	(élla) está (+ fem adj)	*in a good/ bad mood*	de buen / mal humor

Here are some extra adjectives you could use to describe people. Can you decide whether they go with the verb **ser** or **estar**?

good	bueno	*bad*	malo
hard-working	trabajador	*lazy*	vago /perezoso
interesting	interesante	*boring*	aburrido / pesado
quiet	tranquilo	*loud*	ruidoso
strong	fuerte	*weak*	débil
capable	competente	*useless*	inútil
confident	seguro de sí mismo	*nervous*	nervioso
generous	generoso	*mean*	tacaño
helpful	atento	*unhelpful*	poco servicial
odd	raro	*normal*	normal / corriente
polite	cortés	*rude*	descortés / grosero
practical	práctico	*unpractical*	poco práctico
reliable	fiable	*unreliable*	poco fiable
relaxed	relajado	*up-tight*	tenso
sensible	sensato	*stupid*	estúpido
sensitive	sensible	*unfeeling*	insensible
serious	serio	*frivolous*	frívolo
sincere	sincero	*insincere*	insincero / poco sincero
strong-willed	decidido	*weak*	débil
well-behaved	que se porta bien	*badly behaved*	que se porta mal
up-to-date	de moda	*out-of-date*	fuera de moda

the five senses *los cinco sentidos*

sight	la vista	*to see*	ver	*I see*	veo
hearing	el oído	*to hear*	oír	*I hear*	oigo
taste	el gusto	*to taste*	probar	*I taste*	pruebo
smell	el olfato	*to smell*	oler	*I smell*	huelo
touch	el tacto	*to touch*	tocar	*I touch*	toco

Useful phrases

He / She has ...	(Él / Ella) tiene ...
a sense of humour	un sentido de humor
plenty of will power	mucha fuerza de voluntad
a kind-heart	buen corazón
a weakness for ...	debilidad por ...
a good imagination	una buena imaginación

Useful verbs

to get bored	aburrirse	I *am getting bored*	me aburro
to be interested in something	interesarse por algo	I *am interested in ...*	me intereso por ...
to be worried about something	estar preocupado por algo	I *am worried about ...*	me preocupo por ...

Extras

angry	enfadado
annoyed	enojado
kind	amable
unkind	poco amable
laid-back	despreocupado
dynamic	dinámico

Lots of expressions we use in English like *to be hot, cold, hungry, thirsty* and so on are expressed in Spanish using the verb **tener** as in the following table:

to be hot	tener calor	tengo calor	*I am hot*
to be cold	tener frío	tiene frío	*he is cold*
to be hungry	tener hambre	tenemos hambre	*we are hungry*
to be thirsty	tener sed	tienes sed	*you are thirsty*
to be sleepy	tener sueño	tienen sueño	*they are sleepy*
to be in a hurry	tener prisa	tengo prisa	*I am in a hurry*
to be lucky	tener suerte	tiene suerte	*she is lucky*
to be afraid	tener miedo	tienen miedo	*they are afraid*

False friends

You may have noticed a couple of **falsos amigos** *false friends* in this area: This table should help you:

English	Spanish
sensitive	sensible
sensible	sensato
nice, kind	simpático
sympathetic	comprensivo

1.5 My things

Core vocabulary

things	las cosas
bag	el bolso / la bolsa
briefcase	la cartera
cheque book	el talonario de cheques
credit cards	las tarjetas de crédito
diary	la agenda
driving licence	el permiso de conducir
glasses / sunglasses	las gafas (de sol)
keys	las llaves
note book	la libreta / el bloc
passport	el pasaporte
pen	la pluma
purse	el monedero
wallet	la cartera
watch	el reloj

The words for *your* (fam. sing.) / *his* / *her*, *their* / *your* (formal plural) follows the same pattern as the word for **my**, but the pattern for *our* and *your* (fam. plural) is a bit more complex; this is because the former do not have separate feminine forms, whilst the latter do:

my	mi, mis
your (familiar)	tu, tus
his, her,	su, sus
your (formal)	
our	nuestro, nuestra, nuestros, nuestras
your	vuestro, vuestra, vuestros, vuestras
their,	su, sus
your (formal)	

on my desk · *en mi escritorio*

computer	el ordenador
hard drive	el disco duro
mobile	el (teléfono) móvil
mouse	el ratón
laptop	el ordenador portátil
palm-top	el ordenador de bolsillo
PC	el PC
phone	el teléfono
printer	la impresora
scanner	el escáner

at home / *en casa*

at home	*en casa*
DVD	el disco de vídeo polivalente, el DVD
CD	el disco compacto, el CD
CD / DVD player	el lector de CD / DVD
discs	discos
camera	la cámara, la máquina fotográfica
video camera	la cámara de vídeo
digital camera	la cámara digital
film	la película
roll of film	el carrete / rollo
photos	las fotos

my friends / *mis amigos / amigas*

my friends	*mis amigos / amigas*
girl friend(s) (f)	mis amigas
boy friend(s) (m)	mis amigos
girlfriend	mi novia
boyfriend	mi novio
colleagues	mis colegas

Here are a few expressions used in colloquial Spanish:

bike	la bici
TV	la tele
other half	la media naranja
kids	los críos

Useful phrases

Have you got a ... ?	Tienes / tiene usted un(a) ... ?
I have lost my ...	He perdido mi ...
I can't find my ...	No encuentro mi ...
Have you seen my ...	¿Has visto mi ...?

Useful verbs

to lose / mislay	perder
to find	encontrar
to forget	olvidar

1.6 I think, I feel

Core vocabulary

to like	(gustar*)	*liking*	(el gusto)	*I like*	(me gusta)
to love	amar	*love*	el amor	*I love*	amo
to prefer	preferir	*preference*	la preferencia	*I prefer*	prefiero
to dislike	(no gustar)	*dislike*	la antipatía	*I dislike*	(no me gusta)
to hate	odiar	*hate*	el odio	*I hate*	odio

*The verb **gustar** is used to express the idea of liking, but it has to be used back-to-front, because it really means *to please*! So what you really say is *this car pleases me* me gusta este coche. Study the table and learn the examples to help you remember how to use this expression. Note how the person word changes, and that only two verb endings are used, to match the thing or things liked, not the person liking. It really is back to front!

	singular things	**plural things**
I like	me gusta	me gustan
you like (familiar sing.)	te gusta	te gustan
he / she likes		
you like (formal sing.)	le gusta	le gustan
we like	nos gusta	nos gustan
you like (familiar pl.)	os gusta	os gustan
they like		
you like (formal pl.)	les gusta	les gustan

I like wine	me gusta el vino
you like beer	te gusta la cerveza
he likes football	le gusta el fútbol
we like Spain	nos gusta España
you like working	os gusta trabajar
they like travelling	les gusta viajar
I like tomatoes	me gustan los tomates
you like oranges	te gustan las naranjas
she likes sweets	le gustan los caramelos
we like Spanish people	nos gustan los españoles
you like public holidays	os gustan las fiestas
they like holidays	les gustan las vacaciones

to believe	creer	*belief*	la creencia	*I believe*	creo
to think	pensar	*thought*	el pensamiento	*I think*	pienso
to feel	sentirse	*feeling*	el sentimiento	*I feel*	me siento
to worry	preocuparse	*worry*	la preocupación	*I worry*	me preocupo
to advise	aconsejar	*advice*	el consejo	*I advise*	aconsejo
to encourage	animar	*encouragement*	el ánimo	*I encourage*	animo
to exaggerate	exagerar	*exaggeration*	la exageración	*I am exaggerating*	exagero
to joke	bromear	*joke*	la brioma	*I am joking*	hablo en broma
to lie	mentir	*lie*	la mentira	*I am lying*	miento
to promise	prometer	*promise*	la promesa	*I promise*	prometo

Note that **aconsejar** and **animar** need a subjunctive verb after them if there is a subordinate clause (see p. 23). The same is true of **creer** and **pensar** when used in the negative

te aconsejo que no vayas	*I advise you not to go*
le voy a animar a que trabaje	*I am going to encourage him to work*
no creo que esté allí	*I don't believe he is there*
no pienso que tengan miedo	*I don't think they are afraid*

Useful verbs

Negative and positive experiences

to be disappointed	estar desilusionado	to be relieved	estar aliviado
to be depressed	estar deprimido	to be lucky	tener suerte
to be stressed	estar estresado	to be elated	estar eufórico
to be discouraged	estar desanimado	to be relaxed	estar relajado
to be embarrassed	estar avergonzado	to be encouraged	estar animado
to be nervous	estar nervioso	to be at ease	estar a gusto
to be worried	estar preocupado	to be confident	estar seguro
to be sad	estar triste	to be reassured	estar tranquilo
to be ashamed	estar avergonzado	to be happy	estar contento
to be unfortunate	tener mala suerte	to be proud	estar orgulloso
		to be fortunate	ser afortunado

Verbs which are used with another verb

to want to	querer	*I want to go*	quiero ir
to be able to	poder	*I can go in*	puedo entrar
to have to	tener que	*I must leave*	tengo que irme
to need to	necesitar	*I need to go out*	necesito salir
to 'ought' to	deber	*I should stay at home*	debería quedarme en casa

What is it like?

acceptable	aceptable	*comfortable*	cómodo
considerable	considerable	*probable*	probable
possible	posible	*preferable*	preferible
remarkable	extraordinario	*responsible*	responsable
tolerable	tolerable		

Most words which end in **–able** or **-ible** are the same in English and in Spanish, but in Spanish remember to pronounce the vowels clearly and to stress the **a** of **-able** or the **i** of **-ible**.

1.7 Expressing an opinion

Core vocabulary

to believe	creer
to consider	considerar
to think	pensar
to agree/ disagree	estar de acuerdo / no estar de acuerdo
to argue	discutir / pelearse
to ask	preguntar
to dispute	disputar
to question	cuestionar
to quote	citar
to request	pedir
to suggest	sugerir

to compare	comparar	*I compare*	comparo
to contrast	contrastar	*I contrast*	contrasto
to differ	diferir	*I differ*	difiero
to discuss	discutir	*I discuss*	discuto
to conclude	concluir	*I conclude*	concluyo

firstly	primero / en primer lugar
secondly	segundo / en segundo lugar
finally	finalmente / por último
actually	efectivamente / en realidad
basically	básicamente / fundamentalmente
clearly	evidentemente
consequently	por consecuencia
fortunately / unfortunately	afortunadamente / desafortunadamente
generally	generalmente
honestly	francamente
mainly	principalmente
normally	normalmente
obviously	obviamente
particularly	especialmente
principally	principalmente
really	verdaderamente
usually / unusually	normalmente / excepcionalmente

Useful phrases

in my / his / her opinion	en mi / su / opinión
above all	sobre todo
although	aunque
as a result	como resultado
as well as	además de
however	sin embargo
in many respects	en muchos respectos / sentidos
in spite of	a pesar de
instead of	en lugar de
nevertheless	no obstante
otherwise	de lo contrario
similarly	igualmente
the reason is	es porque
to tell the truth	a decir verdad
I wish I could agree	ojalá pudiera estar de acuerdo
I beg to differ	siento tener que disentir
I mean	quiero decir
I maintain	mantengo / sostengo
for example	por ejemplo
etc.	etcétera
in brief	en breve

the advantages / disadvantages are	las ventajas / desventajas son
the pros and cons	los pros y los contras
to conclude	para concluir
bad / good	malo / bueno
comfortable / uncomfortable	cómodo / incómodo
better / worse	mejor / peor
nice / not very nice	agradable / desgradable
too hard / easy	demasiado difícil / fácil

1.8 I do (I + useful action verbs) *hago*

Useful verbs

to wake up	despertarse	I wake up	me despierto
to get up	levantarse	I get up	me levanto
to take a shower	ducharse	I take a shower	me ducho
to get dressed	vestirse	I get dressed	me visto
to eat	comer	I eat	como
to drink	beber	I drink	bebo
to work	trabajar	I work	trabajo
to go home	regresar / volver (a casa)	I go home	regreso / vuelvo a casa
to play	jugar	I play	juego
to watch television	ver la tele(visión)	I watch	veo la tele(visión)
to read	leer	I read	leo
to get washed	lavarse	I get washed	me lavo
to go to bed	acostarse	I go to bed	me acuesto
to laugh	reír	I laugh	río
to smile	sonreír	I smile	sonrío
to giggle	reírse tontamente	I giggle	me río tontamente
to sleep	dormir	I sleep	duermo
to dream	soñar	I dream	sueño

coming and going verbs *verbos de ir y venir*

to walk	andar	I walk	voy andando
to run	correr	I run	corro
to ride	montar / ir en/a	I ride	monto / voy en / a
to drive	conducir / llevar el coche	I drive	conduzco / llevo el coche

to *arrive*	llegar	I *arrive*	llego
to *depart*	irse (person), salir (e.g. train)	I *depart*	me voy / salgo
to *enter*	entrar	I *enter*	entro
to *leave*	salir	I *leave*	salgo
to *come*	venir	I *come*	vengo
to *go*	ir	I *go*	voy
to *go up*	subir	I *go up*	subo
to *go down*	bajar	I *go down*	bajo
to *stay*	quedar	I *stay*	quedo
to *return*	volver	I *return*	vuelvo

communicating — *comunicar*

to *speak*	hablar
to *repeat something*	repetir algo
to *talk to someone*	hablar con alguien
to *whisper to someone*	susurrar a alguien
to *shout at someone*	gritar a alguien
to *ask a question*	hacer una pregunta / preguntar
to *ask for something*	pedir algo
to *respond to a question*	contestar / responder
to *tell a story*	contar un cuento
to *enjoy yourself*	divertirse
to *get angry*	enfadarse
to *have trouble / difficulty*	tener dificultad(es)
to *get depressed*	ponerse deprimido/a
to *know / meet someone*	conocer a alguien
to *know something*	saber algo
to *cheat*	estafar
to *trick*	engañar
to *challenge*	desafiar
to *compliment*	felicitar
to *neglect*	descuidar

Useful phrases

Spanish also uses a number of impersonal expressions with similar sorts of meaning. There are a number of impersonal expressions in Spanish which consist of an adjective followed by an infinitive.

it's necessary	es necesario llegar a las diez	*it's necessary to arrive at ten*
it's vital	es imprescindible hacerlo	*it's vital to do it*
it's obligatory	es obligatorio pagar la cuenta	*it's obligatory to pay the bill*
it's possible	es posible salir	*it's possible to go out*
it's impossible	es imposible saber	*it's impossible to know*
it's dangerous	es peligroso bañarse aquí	*it's dangerous to swim here*
it's horrible	es horrible verle así	*it's horrible to see him like this*
it's prohibited	está prohibido fijar carteles	*it's prohibited to put up posters*

1.9 Don't panic!

Core vocabulary

Help!	¡Socorro!
Listen!	¡Escucha / escuche!
Danger	Peligro
Watch out!	¡Cuidado!
Warning	aviso / advertencia
No entry	Prohibido entrar / la entrada

Useful phrases

Do you understand me?	¿Me comprende(s) / entiende(s)?
Do you understand?	¿Comprende(s)?
Can you help me?	¿Puede(s) ayudarme?
Do you speak English?	¿Habla(s) inglés?
Can you say it more slowly?	Dilo / dígalo más despacio.
I didn't catch what you said.	No oí lo que dijiste / dijo.
Please can you find someone who speaks English?	¿Puede(s) buscar a alguien que hable inglés?
Can you write it down for me please?	¿Puede(s) escribirlo, por favor?
How do you spell it?	¿Cómo se escribe?
Have you got the phone number for the ...?	¿Tiene(s) el número de teléfono de ...?
police	la policía
fire brigade	los bomberos

ambulance	la ambulancia
doctor	el médico
breakdown services	los servicios de asistencia en carretera
What do I need to dial first?	¿Qué tengo que marcar primero?
What is the code for...?	¿Cuál es el prefijo de / para ...?
How do I get an outside line?	¿Cómo puedo obtener una línea exterior?

02

family

2.1 My family

Core vocabulary

my family and relatives	*mi familia y mis parientes / familiares*
my mother	mi madre
my father	mi padre
my parents	mis padres
my sister	mi hermana
my brother	mi hermano
my younger brother	mi hermano menor
my younger sister	mi hermana menor
my older brother	mi hermano mayor
my older sister	mi hermana mayor
my half-brother	mi hermanastro
my half-sister	mi hermanastra
twin brother	mi hermano gemelo
twin sister	mi hermana gemela
my grandmother	mi abuela
my grandfather	mi abuelo
my grandparents	mis abuelos
my great-grandparents	mis bisabuelos
my grandson	mi nieto
my granddaughter	mi nieta
my uncle	mi tío
my aunt	mi tía
my cousin (m)	mi primo
my cousin (f)	mi prima
my nephew	mi sobrino
my niece	mi sobrina
my husband	mi marido
my wife	mi mujer / esposa
my ex-husband	mi ex-marido
my ex-wife	mi ex-mujer
my father-in-law	mi suegro
my mother-in-law	mi suegra
my brother-in-law	mi cuñado
my sister-in-law	mi cuñada
my partner	mi pareja
my friend	mi amigo/a
my boyfriend m	mi novio
my girlfriend	mi novia
my godson	mi ahijado
my goddaughter	mi ahijada

a married couple	un matrimonio
widow	la viuda
widower	el viudo

Useful phrases

May I introduce my	Te presento a mi ... / Éste/a es mi ...
Pleased to meet you.	¡Encantado! / ¡Mucho gusto!
I am sorry to hear about your separation/ divorce / bereavement	Lamento lo de tu / su separación / divorcio / pérdida
Will you go out with me?	¿Quieres salir conmigo?
I am going out with ...	Salgo con ...
We are just good friends ...	Somos amigos nada más

Useful verbs

to like someone	gustar*
to flirt	ligar
to kiss	besar
to go out with someone	salir con alguien
to get on with someone	llevarse bien con alguien
to have a good time	divertirse
to have intercourse / sex	tener relaciones sexuales
to get married	casarse
to get on each other's nerves	ponerse los nervios de punta
to look after someone	cuidar de
to quarrel	pelearse
to separate	separarse
to divorce	divorciarse

*see p. 57

pet names / nombres de cariño

darling	querido/a
darling (for a woman only)	nena
sweetheart	cariño, mi amor
honey	mi vida
daddy	papaíto
mummy	mamaíta
grandpa	abuelito
grandma, nan	abuelita
kiddy	chiquillo/a

Tips for remembering words

- Remember that lots of words for family members can be grouped in similar pairs – **hermano/a, hijo/a** and so on.
- Try to associate the words with members of your own family – you could draw your own family tree and label it.
- Think of **padre** as being a word we use for a *priest* (Father ...) and as being related to our word *paternal* similarly with **madre** and *maternal*.

2.2 Children

Core vocabulary

baby	el bebé
infant	el niño / la niña
child	el niño / la niña
boy	el muchacho / el chico
girl	la muchacha / la chica
twin	el gemelo / la gemela
teenager	el adolescente / joven
adolescent	el / la adolescente
pregnancy	el embarazo
birth	el nacimiento
newborn baby	el recién nacido
nanny	la niñera
childminder	la niñera
babysitter	el canguro
midwife	la comadrona
crèche	la guardería
playschool	el jardín de infancia
baby's bottle	el biberón
teat	la tetina
dummy	el chupete
bib	el babero
babymilk	la leche para niños
high chair	la silla alta
nappy	el pañal
carrycot	el moisés
cot	la cuna
pram	el cochecito (de niño)
pushchair	la sillita de paseo
toy	el juguete

wind	el flato
colic	el cólico
an only child	un hijo único / la hija única
an adopted child	un niño adoptado
an orphan	un huérfano
children's playground	el patio de recreo
swing	el columpio
slide	el tobogán
roundabout	el carrusel

Useful verbs

to be expecting a baby	estar encinta
to breastfeed	amamantar, criar a los pechos
to burp	eructar
to change a nappy	cambiar un pañal
to cry	llorar
to feed	dar de comer
to give a bottle	dar el biberón
to rock	acunar, mecer
to teethe	echar los dientes
to look after	cuidar a
to babysit	hacer de canguro

Useful phrases

I am pregnant	Estoy embarazada.
It's a boy / girl.	Es un niño / una niña.
sibling rivalry	la rivalidad entre hermanos
family planning	la planificación familiar
a spoilt child	un niño mimado

I need ... — *necesito ...*

a cream for a sore bottom	una crema para un culito dolorido
sun cream for children	un bronceador para niños
shampoo for children	un champú para niños
something for wind	algo para flato
something for children teething	algo para la dentición

Word-building

You may notice that often one word will have another word or
words based on it; here are some examples:

child	el niño	la niñera	*nanny*
to drink	beber	el biberón	*baby's bottle*
chair	silla	sillita	*little chair*
to watch over	guardar	guardería	*crèche*

2.3 Anniversaries, marriage and death

Core vocabulary

birthday	el cumpleaños
engagement	el noviazgo
marriage	el matrimonio
death	la muerte
the wedding	la boda
church	la iglesia
town hall	el ayuntamiento
engagement ring	el anillo de compromiso
wedding invitation	la invitación de boda
wedding day	el día de la boda
bride	la novia
bridegroom	el novio
bridesmaid	la dama de honor
wedding dress	el traje de novia
wedding ceremony	la ceremonia nupcial
wedding ring	el anillo de boda
wedding certificate	el certificado nupcial
wedding cake	el pastel de la boda
honeymoon	la luna de miel
married life	la vida matrimonial
separation	la separación
divorce	el divorcio
heterosexual	heterosexual
homosexual	homosexual
lesbian	lesbiana
death	la muerte
funeral	el funeral
corpse	el cadáver

coffin	el ataúd
cemetery	el cementerio
burial	el entierro
cremation	la cremación
grave	la sepultura
death duties	el impuesto de sucesiones
death certificate	la partida de defunción
will	el testamento

Useful verbs

to get engaged	prometerse
to get married	casarse
to die	morir
to be buried	ser enterrado
to be in mourning	estar de luto
to commit suicide	suicidarse

Useful phrases

Congratulations!	¡Felicitaciones!
Happy birthday	Feliz cumpleaños
Merry Christmas	Feliz Navidad
Happy New Year	Feliz Año Nuevo
Congratulations on your	Felicitaciones por tu
engagement	noviazgo
wedding	boda
anniversary	aniversario

We would like to wish you every future happiness.	Os / les deseamos la más completa felicidad para el futuro.
We would like to send you our best wishes.	Os / les mandamos la enhorabuena.
I would like to convey my condolences.	Te / le acompaño en el sentimiento.
I am very sorry to learn of your sad loss.	Quiero expresar mi tristeza por tu / su pérdida.

03

work

3.1 Job titles

Core vocabulary

accountant	el contable (m+f)
actor / actress	el actor / la actriz
architect	el arquitecto
builder	el albañil (m+f)
businessman	el hombre de negocios
businesswoman	la mujer de negocios
civil servant	el funcionario (del estado)
computer operator	el operador de ordenador
computer programmer	el programador de ordenadores
dentist	el dentista
doctor	el médico
driver	el conductor
electrician	el electricista (m+f)
engineer	el ingeniero
farmer	el granjero
fireman	el bombero
hairdresser	el peluquero
journalist	el periodista (m+f)
lawyer	el abogado
lecturer / professor	el profesor
mechanic	el mecánico
musician	el músico
nurse	el enfermero / la enfermera
plumber	el fontanero
police officer	el guardia / policía (m+f)
postman	el cartero
receptionist	el recepcionista (m+f)
scientist	el científico
secretary	el secretario / la secretaria
shop assistant	el dependiente / la dependienta
shop keeper	el tendero
student	el estudiante
waiter / waitress	el camarero / la camarera
unemployed	desempleado / parado
retired	jubilado

The feminine form will usually be the same but will end in –a, except for words ending in –e, which don't change, and a few odd ones marked (m+f).

the staff	el personal
chairman	el presidente
chief executive	el director
managing director	el director / gerente
director	el director
company secretary	el administrador de empresa
departmental head	el jefe de departamento
accountant	el contable
manager	el gerente
business consultant	el asesor comercial
personal assistant	el ayudante personal
employer	el empleador / empresario
employee	el empleado
sales representative	el representante / viajante
secretary	el secretario / la secretaria
caretaker	el conserje
cleaner	el encargado de la limpieza
trainee	el aprendiz
work experience	la experiencia laboral

I would like to work in / I work in / I used to work in

I'd like to work as / in...	me gustaría trabajar de / en …
I work as / in	trabajo en / de …
I used to work as / in	trabajaba en / de
agriculture	la agricultura
banking	la banca
building trade	la industria de la construcción
catering	la hostelería
civil service	la administración pública
commerce	el comercio
finance	las finanzas
the hotel industry	el sector hotelero
insurance	el seguro
leisure services	el ocio
manufacturing	la fabricación
medicine	la medicina
the media	los medios de comunicación de masa
the public services	los servicios públicos
purchasing	la compra
retail	la venta al por menor
service industry	el sector de servicios

show business	el mundo del espectáculo
textiles	la industria textil
tourism	el turismo
transport	el transporte
wholesale	la venta al por mayor

Useful verbs

to work / earn my living	trabajar / ganarme la vida
to be out of work	estar desempleado / en paro
to buy / sell	comprar / vender
to import / export	importar / exportar
to manage	dirigir, gestionar
to manufacture	fabricar

- In Spain, many 'state' jobs fall into the category of **funcionario**; for these and the majority of professions, entry and promotion are usually by **oposiciones** – competitive exams; these can take several years to prepare for, and some people will take them several times before getting the type of job they want.
- In many state jobs, you have to go where the appropriate government department sends you.
- Spain has had a minimum salary level for many years which is known as the **salario mínimo interprofesional**.

You can build up your vocabulary by learning a cluster of words:

work	el trabajo
to work	trabajar
hard working	trabajador
worker	el trabajador
worker (f)	la trabajadora
employment	el empleo
unemployment	el desempleo
employer	el empleador / empresario
employee	el empleado
to employ	emplear
employed	empleado
unemployed	desempleado
manager	gerente
to manage	gestionar
management	gestión
manageable	gestionable

3.2 Where do you work?

Core vocabulary

I work in a ...	***trabajo en ...***
bank	un banco
building site	una obra
factory	una fábrica
farm	una granja
garage	un garaje
hospital	un hospital
hotel	un hotel
mine	una mina
office	una oficina
post office	(oficina de) correos
restaurant	un restaurante
school	una escuela
service station	una estación de servicio
shopping centre	un centro comercial
studio	un estudio
town hall	el ayuntamiento
workshop	un taller

3.3 The office

the company	la compañía / empresa
headquarters	la oficina central
subsidiary	la filial
firm	la firma / empresa
limited company	la sociedad anónima / limitada
the premises	el local
boardroom	la sala de juntas
canteen	la cantina / el comedor
meeting room	la sala de conferencias
reception	la recepción
entrance	la entrada
exit	la salida
security code	el código de seguridad
pass	el pase / permiso
switchboard	la central
mail	el correo
extension	el interno

I work in the ... department	trabajo en el departamento de ...
accounts	contabilidad
administration	administración
advertising	publicidad
after-sales	posventa
catering	hostelería
distribution	distribución
export	exportación
import	importación
facilities management	gestión de servicios
information technology	informática
insurance	seguro
legal	legal
manufacturing	fabricación
marketing	mercadeo / márketing
personnel / human resources	personal / recursos humanos
property	propiedades
purchasing	compras
sales	ventas
technical	técnico

Useful verbs

to buy	comprar	compro
to manage	dirigir	dirijo
to manufacture	fabricar	fabrico
to research	investigar	investigo
to sell	vender	vendo
to study	estudiar	estudio
to travel	viajar	viajo
to work	trabajar	trabajo

Useful phrases

Where do you work?	¿Dónde trabaja usted?
Which department do you work in?	¿En qué departamento trabaja usted?
Our head office is based in ...	Nuestra sede central está en ...
Can I get you a coffee?	¿Le puedo traer un café?
Would you like to meet ...?	¿Le gustaría conocer a ...?

3.4 Conditions of employment

working conditions	las condiciones de trabajo
the working day	el día laboral
the working week	la semana laboral
holidays	las vacaciones
annual holiday	las vacaciones anuales
national holidays	las fiestas nacionales
pay	el sueldo
salary	el salario
income	los ingresos
income tax	los impuestos sobre la renta
VAT	el impuesto de valor añadido
applicant	el aspirante / candidato
application	la solicitud
application form	la solicitud
CV	el currículum (vitae)
contract	el contrato
job interview	la entrevista de trabajo
full-time job	el empleo a tiempo completo
part-time job	el empleo a tiempo parcial
office hours	las horas de oficina
overtime	las horas extra(s)
flexitime	el horario flexible
coffee break	el descanso (para tomar café)
lunch-time	la hora del almuerzo
meeting	la reunión
union	el sindicato
union meeting	la reunión sindical
strike	la huelga
demand	la demanda
leave	el permiso
sick leave	el permiso por enfermedad
sick note	el justificante por enfermedad
compassionate leave	el permiso por motivos familiares
dismissal	el despedido
redundancy	el desempleo
bankruptcy	la quiebra
laying off	el despido
standard of living	el nivel de vida
unemployment rate	la tasa de paro / desempleo

Useful phrases

It is stressful / stimulating.	es estresante / estimulante.
He / she is very	Es muy
efficient.	eficiente.
organized / disorganized.	organizado / desorganizado.
hard working / lazy.	trabajador/ perezoso.

Verbs

to be behind with one's work	estar atrasado en el trabajo
to catch up	alcanzar
to be ahead	ir por delante
to have a deadline	la fecha tope
to be overworked	trabajar demasiado
to be stressed	estar estresado/a

3.5 Writing a letter

- Always write your name / address on the back of the envelope, after the abbreviation **Rte:** (**Remitente** *sender*).
- Only write your town / city and the date at the top right of your letter.
- All familiar letters begin with **Querido/a.**
- After the person's name, use a colon, **Querido Xavier:**

Informal letters

Dear Dad / brother / son / *grandad*	Querido papá / hermano / hijo / abuelito
Dear Mum / sister / daughter */ grandma*	Querida mamá / hermana / hija / abuelita
Dear José / Manuel / Xavier	Querido José / Manuel / Xavier
Dear friend	Querido amigo / amiga
till the next (letter)	Hasta la próxima …
write soon	Escríbe(me) pronto
give my regards to your *father / parents …*	Dale mis recuerdos a tu(s) padre(s) …
give a kiss to your little *brother*	Dale un beso a tu hermanito
A kiss / hug (= love from…)	Un beso / abrazo (de …)

Formal letters

Dear Don Pablo / Mr Blanco	Querido don Pablo / señor Blanco
Dear Doña Lola / Mrs / Miss Morales	Querida doña Lola / señor(it)a Morales
Dear Sir / Madam	Muy señor mío / señora mía
Dear … (very formal)	Estimado/a …
Yours sincerely	(Le saluda) atentamente

3.6 Using the telephone

Core vocabulary

telephone	el teléfono
receiver	el auricular
extension	la extensión
mobile	el (teléfono) móvil
telephone number	el número de teléfono
directory	la guía telefónica
local call	la llamada local
long distance call	la llamada de larga distancia
international call	la llamada internacional

Useful verbs

to phone	llamar por teléfono
to call	llamar
to call back	devolver la llamada
to divert a call	desviar una llamada
to put someone through	pasar
to look up a number	buscar

Useful phrases

Hello!	¡Díga(me)! (answering the phone)
Hello!	¡Oíga(me)! (making a call)
Could I speak to …?	Póngame con …
Can I have extension … please?	Deme la extensión …, por favor
Can I have someone who deals with …?	Póngame con alguien que se encargue de …
Who is calling?	¿Dígame? ¿De parte de quién?

Can you tell me what it is about?	¿Me puede decir de qué se trata?
Who would you like to speak to?	¿Con quién quiere usted hablar?
Speaking!	¡Soy yo!
Can you wait a moment?	Espere un momento.
I am putting you through.	Le estoy pasando.
The line is engaged / busy.	Está comunicando.
The line is free.	La línea está abierta / libre.
Do you want to hold?	¿Quiere esperar?
Would you like to leave a message?	¿Quiere dejar un recado?
Can I take your name and number?	Deme su nombre y su número.
I haven't got a signal	No tengo señal.
My battery is running low.	Mi batería se está agotando.
Can you ring back?	¿Puede volver a llamar?
Can you text me?	¿Puede mandarme un texto?

3.7 Using the computer

Core words

computer	el ordenador
keyboard	el teclado
mouse	el ratón
microphone	el micrófono
speakers	los parlantes
hard drive	el disco duro
screen	la pantalla
laptop	el ordenador portátil
printer	la impresora
scanner	el escáner
e-mail	el e-mail / emilio / correo electrónico
worldwide web	el Web
net	la red
code	el código
password	la contraseña de acceso
programme	el programa
modem	el módem
connector	el conector
battery	la pila (dry) / batería (wet)
phone jack	el enchufe de teléfono

Useful verbs

switch on	encender
type in	escribir
log on	acceder al sistema
log off	salir del sistema
save	guardar / archivar
go on line	conectar
send an e-mail	mandar un e-mail
receive mail	recibir un e-mail
download a file	descargar un fichero / archivo
recharge the battery	recargar

Useful phrases

Have you got a …?	¿Tiene un …?
My computer isn't working.	Mi ordenador no funciona.
Is there anyone who can help me?	¿Hay alguien que pueda ayudarme?

04

education

4.1 Primary and secondary education

The school system

age *edad*	school	*escuela*
2–6	*infant*	parvulario / jardín de infancia
6–14	*middle*	colegio
14–18/19	*upper*	instituto

- A high proportion of Spanish children attend a nursery school.
- Primary and secondary school children follow a national curriculum regulated by the local offices of the Ministry of Education.
- Private sector schools are called **colegio** regardless of the age of the children. The private sector has more freedom over the curriculum and many are religious.
- Spanish school students who fail their end-of-year exams have to spend much of the summer studying at revision lessons to prepare for retakes in September; if they fail these exams, they have to repeat the whole year, and may even do so two or three times.

Core vocabulary

headmaster	el director
deputy head	el vice-director
primary teacher	el maestro
secondary teacher	el profesor
pupil	el alumno / la alumna
the school secretary	el secretario / la secretaria
the school nurse	la enfermera de escuela
the school caretaker	el conserje
lesson	la lección / la clase
break	el recreo
lunch time	el almuerzo
the bell	el timbre
the end of lessons	el fin de la jornada escolar
term	el trimestre
half-term	las vacaciones de mediados del trimestre
holidays	las vacaciones

school hours	el horario lectivo / escolar
progress test	la evaluación
final examination	la reválida
continuous assessment	la evaluación continua
the timetable	el horario
school subjects	las asignaturas
Art	el diseño
Biology	la biología
Chemistry	la química
Civics	la educación cívica
English	el inglés
French	el francés
History	la historia
Geography	la geografía
German	el alemán
Information technology	la informática
Maths	las matemáticas
Music	la música
P.E.	la educación física
Physics	la física
Science	la ciencia
Spanish	el español
Technology	la tecnología
the building	el edificio
the classroom	el aula (f)
the corridor	el pasillo
the science laboratory	el laboratorio de ciencias
the gym	el gimnasio
the games room	la sala de juegos
the sports hall	el polideportivo
the music room	el aula de música
the library	la biblioteca
the computer room	el aula de Informática
the cloakroom	el guardarropa
the changing rooms	los vestuarios
the toilets	los aseos / servicios
the desk	el pupitre
the blackboard	la pizarra
the projector	el proyector
the computer	el ordenador
the white board	la pizarra blanca
the interactive whiteboard	la pizarra blanca interactiva
the overhead projector	el retroproyector

the book	el libro
the exercise book	el cuaderno
the pencil case	el estuche / plumero
the pen	la pluma
the biro / ballpoint	el boli / bolígrafo
the pencil	el lápiz
the eraser	la goma de borrar
the board-rubber	el borrador
the calculator	la calculadora
the protractor	el transportador
the ruler	la regla
the report	el boletín (de notas)
the school bag	el bolso
the sports kit	el equipo de deporte

Useful verbs

to read	leer
to speak	hablar
to listen	escuchar
to talk	hablar
to discuss	discutir
to write	escribir
to copy	copiar
to take notes	tomar apuntes / apuntar
to be quiet	estar / quedar en silencio / callado
to do your homework	hacer los deberes
to get a good mark	sacar buena nota
to sit an exam	pasar un examen
to pass a test	aprobar una prueba
to fail a test	fracasar / suspender una prueba
to re-sit	volver a presentarse / repetir un examen
to repeat a year	repetir el curso

4.2 Further and higher education

- A high proportion of young Spanish people go to university.
- There are more girls at Spanish universities than boys.
- University fees and expenses are considerable, and few students get grants.
- Most Spanish students go to their local university and live at home.

- Many Spanish students do a part-time job to help pay for their education.
- For certain specialized degrees, e.g. medicine, students may go away from home.
- Most degrees start with a general, foundation course; many last five years or more.

Core vocabulary

college	el colegio
technical college	la escuela politécnica / el instituto de formación profesional
university	la universidad
faculty	la facultad
class	la clase
lecture	la clase / conferencia
seminar	el seminario
tutorial	el seminario
professor	el catedrático
student	el estudiante
research student	el estudiante investigador
graduate	el licenciado
undergraduate	el estudiante universitario
apprentice	el aprendiz
trainee	el aprendiz
a paper (research paper)	el ensayo / artículo de investigación
a report	un reportaje / boletín
a dissertation	la tesina
a thesis	la tesis

Useful verbs

to present a paper	presentar una ponencia
to do a sandwich course	combinar los estudios con el trabajo
to study part-time	estudiar a tiempo parcial
to attend evening class	asistir a clases nocturnas
to do work experience	hacer experiencia laboral
to correct	corregir
to discuss	discutir
to explain	explicar
to learn	aprender
to qualify	sacar el título

to register / enrol	matricularse
to study	estudiar
to teach	enseñar
to translate	traducir
to understand	comprender / entender
to do research	hacer investigaciones

False friends

to sit an exam (not *to pass* – as we understand it)	pasar un examen
a school year (not just *a course*)	un curso
training	la formación
a university course (as well as *a career*)	una carrera

05

at home

5.1 The house

Core vocabulary

house	la casa
home	el hogar
appartment	el apartamento
flat	el piso / apartamento
studio	el estudio
block of flats	el bloque (de pisos)
the building	el edificio
floor / storey	el piso / la planta
ground floor	la planta baja
first floor	el primer piso
second floor	el segundo piso
basement	el sótano
attic	el desván / la buhardilla
stairs	la escalera
lift	el ascensor
garage	el garaje / la cochera
cellar	el sótano / la bodega
cottage	la casita / la choza
farm	la granja
detached house	el chalé / chalet
villa	la villa / casa de campo
council flat	el piso de protección oficial
semi-detached house	la casa adosada
terraced house	la casa adosada
central heating	la calefacción
double glazing	el doble acristalamiento
gas	el gas
electricity	la electricidad
oil	el aceite
water	el agua
services	los servicios públicos
telephone	el teléfono
mains sewerage	el alcantarillado / la cloaca
septic tank	la fosa séptica
sound proofing	la insonorización
insulation	el aislamiento térmico
shutters	las contraventanas
burglar alarm	la alarma antirrobo

outside	fuera
balcony	el balcón
roof	el techo / tejado
slates	las tejas / pizarras
terrace	la terraza
conservatory	el invernadero
garden	el jardín
gate	la puerta / verja
path	el sendero
lawn	el césped
flower bed	el arriate / parterre
vegetable garden	la huerta / el huerto
greenhouse	el invernadero
the situation	la situación / ubicación
aspect	el aspecto
view	la vista / el panorama
swimming pool	la piscina
barbecue	la barbacoa
tennis court	la pista de tenis
stone	la piedra
brick	el ladrillo
timber	la madera
concrete	el hormigón

Useful verbs

to buy	comprar
to sell	vender
to view (a house)	ver
to make an appointment	concertar una cita
to lock up	cerrar con llave

Useful phrases

it overlooks the bay	tiene vistas a / da a la bahía
a central position	una situación central
close to all services	cerca de todos los servicios
in the town centre	en el centro urbano / del pueblo
in the suburbs	en los suburbios
in the country	en el campo

5.2 Rooms

Core vocabulary

room	la habitación / el cuarto
entrance	el vestíbulo
kitchen	la cocina
dining room	el comedor
sitting room	el cuarto de estar / el salón / el living
bedroom	el dormitorio
playroom	el cuarto de juego
bathroom	el cuarto de baño
cloakroom (downstairs toilet)	el lavabo
study / office	el despacho
shower	la ducha
hall	el vestíbulo
landing	el descansillo
stairs	la escalera
utility room	la trascocina
junk room	el trastero
window	la ventana
radiator	el radiador
floor	el suelo
ceiling	el techo
door	la puerta
wall	la pared
windowsill	el altepecho (de la ventana)
central heating	la calefacción
water heater	el calentador de agua
gas	el gas
electricity	la electricidad
oil	el aceite
double glazing	el doble acristalamiento
lock	la cerradura
key	la llave
plug	el enchufe
socket	el enchufe / la toma de corriente
switch	el interruptor
handle	el mango
fuse box	la caja de fusibles
fuse	el fusible
fuse wire	el hilo fusible
torch	la linterna

curtains	las cortinas
blinds	las persianas
shutters	las contraventanas
carpet	la alfombra / la moqueta (fitted)
rug	el tapete / la alfombrilla
floor tiles	las baldosas
wall tiles	los azulejos
flooring	la solería
wallpaper	el papel pintado
paint	la pintura
paintbrush	la brocha (*decorating*) / el pincel (*art*)
ladder	la escalera de mano

Useful verbs

to turn / switch on	encender
to turn / switch off	apagar

Useful phrases

upstairs	arriba
downstairs	abajo
on the first floor	en el primer piso
in the basement	en el sótano
in the attic	en la buhardilla / el desván
Where is the ...?	¿dónde está el / la ... ?
How does it work?	¿cómo funciona?

5.3 Furniture

Core vocabulary

furniture	los muebles
sitting room	el salón
armchair	la butaca
easy chair	el sillón
sofa	el sofá
coffee table	la mesita (para servir el café)
bookcase	la librería / estantería
lamp	la lámpara
pictures	los cuadros

bedroom	el dormitorio
bed	la cama
bedside table	la mesilla de noche
chair	la silla
wardrobe	el armario
chest of drawers	la cómoda
mirror	el espejo
built-in cupboard	el armario empotrado
shelves	los estantes
bathroom	el cuarto de baño
bath	el baño / la bañera
mirror	el espejo
razor	la afeitadora
shower	la ducha
wash basin	el lavabo
toilet	el lavabo / baño / servicio
toilet (bowl)	el retrete / wáter
taps	los grifos
plug	el tapón

5.4 Household goods

Core vocabulary

television	el televisor
video recorder	el aparato de vídeo
DVD player	el lector de disco de vídeo digital, DVD
remote control	el mando a distancia
stereo	el estéreo
radio	la radio
flatscreen television	el televisor a pantalla plana
bedding	la ropa de cama
pillow / pillowcase	la almohada / la funda de almohada
quilt	el edredón
quilt cover	la funda de edredón
sheet	la sábana
fitted sheet	la sábana de cuatro picos
shampoo	el champú
conditioner	el suavizante / acondicionador
hairdryer	el secador de pelo
soap	el jabón
towel	la toalla

deodorant	el desodorante
toothbrush	el cepillo de dientes
toothpaste	la pasta de dientes
vacuum cleaner	la aspiradora
duster	el trapo
brush	el cepillo
dustpan	el cogedor
cleaning materials	los materiales de limpieza
scrubbing brush	el cepillo de fregar
floor mop	la fregona
detergent	el detergente

Useful phrases

Where is the ...?	¿dónde está el / la ...?
It's	está
on the table	en / encima de la mesa
under the bed	debajo de la cama
in the armchair	en la butaca
in the cupboard / drawer	en el armario
Can I have a clean ....?	Me puede dar un/a … limpio/a?
How does the (television) work?	¿Cómo funciona (el televisor)?

Useful verbs

to do housework	hacer las tareas de la casa
to wash	lavar
to clean	limpiar
to vacuum	pasar el aspirador
to make the beds	hacer la cama

5.5 In the kitchen

Core vocabulary

in the kitchen	en la cocina
table	la mesa
chair	la silla
stool	el taburete
drawer	el cajón
cupboard	el armario
shelf	el estante

sink	la pila
fridge	la nevera
dishwasher	el lavaplatos / lavavajillas
washing machine	la lavadora
tumble drier	la secadora
mixer	la batidora
liquidizer	la licuadora
plate	el plato
dinner plate	el plato llano
bowl	el tazón / el plato
salad bowl	la fuente
dish	el plato / la fuente
cup	la taza
saucer	el platillo
mug	el tazón
jug	el jarro / la jarra
teapot	la tetera
sugar bowl	la azucarera
knife	el cuchillo
fork	el tenedor
spoon	la cuchara
teaspoon	la cucharita
soup spoon	la cuchara sopera
dessert spoon	la cuchara de postre
carving knife	el cuchillo de trinchar
bread knife	el cuchillo para cortar pan
vegetable knife	el cuchillo para cortar legumbres
salt	la sal
pepper	la pimienta
mustard	la mostaza
glass	el vaso
wineglass	la copa
champagne glass	la copa de champán
water glass	el vaso
tumbler	el vaso
rubbish	la basura
left-overs	las sobras
packaging	el material de envasado
plastic bags	las bolsas de plástico
kitchen bin / waste bin	el cubo de la basura
bin liner	la bolsa de la basura

dustbin	el cubo de la basura
recycling	el reciclaje
bottle bank	el contenedor de vidrio
compost	el compost

Useful phrases

| I *like / dislike cooking.* | (No) me gusta cocinar. |
| I'll *do the washing up.* | Voy a lavar los platos. |

Useful verbs

In recipes, instructions are usually given using the infinitive form of the verb.

cooking terms	*los términos de cocina*
mix	mezclar
beat	batir
roast	asar
toast	tostar
bake	cocer (al horno)
boil	hervir
steam	cocer al vapor
grill	asar a la parrilla
barbecue	asar a la parrilla
peel	pelar
cut	cortar
slice	cortar en lonchas / tajadas / rodajas / trozos
chop	picar

5.6 Outside

Core vocabulary

garage	la cochera
shed	el cobertizo
footpath	el sendero / la vereda
gate	la verja
security code	el código de (la) seguridad
in the garden	en el jardín
flower bed	el arriate / parterre
lawn	el césped

flower	la flor
plant	la planta
bush / shrub	el arbusto
tree	el árbol
grass	la hierba
weeds	las malas hierbas
herbs	las hierbas finas
bulbs	el bulbo

trees — *los árboles*

beech	la haya
chestnut	el castaño
elm	el olmo
hazel	el avellano
holly	el acebo
oak	el roble
sycamore	el sicomoro
willow	el sauce
poplar	el álamo / chopo
strawberry tree	el madroño (*part of symbol of Madrid*)

flowers — *las flores*

carnation	el clavel
daffodil	el narciso
rose	la rosa
sweet pea	el guisante de olor / clarín
tulip	el tulipán
mimosa	la mimosa
orange-blossom	el azahar

garden tools — *los útiles de jardinería*

fork	la horca / horquilla
hoe	la azada
rake	el rastrillo
spade	la pala
trowel	el desplantador
lawnmower	el cortacésped
wheelbarrow	la carretilla
garden tractor	el tractor de jardín
garden cultivator / rotavator	la cultivadora
hose	la manguera
sprinkler	el aspersor
watering can	la regadera
weedkiller	la herbicida
fertilizer	el fertilizante

insects and pests	**los insectos y los animales dañinos**
ant	la hormiga
bee	la abeja
greenfly	el pulgón
housefly	la mosca
mosquito	el mosquito
spider	la araña
wasp	la avispa

garden furniture	**los muebles de jardín**
barbecue	la parrilla
table	la mesa
deck chair	la tumbona
lounger	la tumbona
bench	el banco
swing	el columpio
slide	el tobogán

Useful phrases

It needs to be weeded.	Hace falta desherbarlo.
It needs to be watered.	Hace falta regarlo.
The grass needs to be cut.	Hace falta cortar el césped / la hierba.
They are ripe / not ripe.	(No) están maduros/as.
I like / dislike gardening.	(No) me gusta la jardinería.
He / she has green fingers.	Se le dan muy bien las plantas.
I am allergic to ...	Soy alérgico/a a ...
I have been stung!	¡Me ha picado!

Useful verbs

to dig	cavar
to plant	plantar
to grow	cultivar (what gardener does)
to weed	desherbar
to water	regar
to pick	(re)coger
to cut the grass	cortar la hierba

5.7 Tools and DIY

Core vocabulary

DIY	el bricolaje
tools	las herramientas
drill	el taladro
(drill) bits	las brocas
hammer	el martillo
pincers	las pinzas
pliers	los alicates
saw	la sierra
chain saw	la sierra de cadena
screwdriver	el destornillador
spanner	la llave de tuercas
staple gun	la grapadora
tape measure	la cinta métrica
nail	el clavo
bolt	el tornillo
nut	la tuerca
staple	la grapa
brush	el cepillo
paint brush	la brocha
scissors	las tijeras
sandpaper	el papel de lija
ladder	la escalera de mano
scaffold	el andamio
tiles (roof)	las tejas
slates	las pizarras
windowpane	el cristal / vidrio
window frame	el marco de ventana
sliding window	la ventana corrediza
shutters	las contraventanas

plumbing and electricity	***las tuberías y la electricidad***
pipe	el tubo / caño
tap	el grifo
wire	el alambre
fuse	el fusible
plug	el enchufe
socket	el enchufe

Useful phrases

Can you fix it?	¿Puedes / puede usted arreglarlo?
Yes I can!	¡Claro que sí!
to fix something to a wall	clavar / fijar algo en la pared
to fix /mend	arreglar / reparar

Useful verbs

to screw	atornillar
to unscrew	destornillar
to hammer	clavar / martillar
to nail	clavar
to drill	taladrar / perforar
to fasten	sujetar
to cut	cortar
to rub down (sandpaper)	lijar
to paint	pintar
to plane	cepillar
to glue	pegar
to solder	soldar
to weld	soldar

06
entertaining and food

6.1 Parties and celebrations

Core vocabulary

Congratulations!	¡Felicitaciones! / ¡Enhorabuena!
a party	una fiesta
a birthday	un cumpleaños
an anniversary	un aniversario
an engagement	un compromiso / noviazgo
a wedding	una boda
a celebration	una celebración / un festejo
silver wedding	las bodas de plata
golden wedding	las bodas de oro
an invitation	una invitación
a reply	una respuesta
an acceptance	una aceptación
a refusal	una denegación
an excuse	una excusa
a thank you letter	una carta de gratitud
a cake	un pastel / una tarta
champagne	champán
a toast	un brindis
a present	un regalo
Cheers!	¡Salud!

Useful phrases

Let's have a party.	Vamos a dar una fiesta.
Let's dance.	Vamos a bailar. / Bailemos.
I would like to propose a toast.	Quisiera proponer un brindis.
I would like to thank our hosts.	Quisiera darles las gracias a nuestros huéspedes.
I've got a hangover.	Tengo una resaca.

Useful verbs

to party	irse de juerga
to eat	comer
to drink	beber
to toast (the bride)	proponer un brindis por la novia
to enjoy oneself	divertirse
to overindulge	excederse

to *have too much to drink*	abusar del alcohol
to *get drunk*	emborracharse
to *feel sick*	marearse

6.2 Mealtimes

- Breakfast (**el desayuno**) is light – it usually comprises coffee, fruit juice, a pastry, biscuits or toast; children often have chocolate spread on bread or toast; cereals and milk are becoming increasingly popular.
- Many people go out from work to a bar midmorning for coffee and a bun or **churros** – these are thin, crispy, finger-doughnuts, dunked in coffee or hot chocolate.
- Lunch (**el almuerzo**) is the main meal of the day; any time from about 1 to 3 p.m.; it usually comprises two or three courses, beginning with a starter or fish, then the main course with vegetables or salad served separately, and often fruit for dessert. The meal is often accompanied by wine, especially at weekends, and is often followed by a **siesta** if time permits.
- **La merienda** is a teatime snack often eaten by children and may consist of a cake or chocolate with a drink.
- Dinner (**la cena**) is served any time from about 9 p.m. to midnight. It is usually a lighter meal than lunch, unless it is a special occasion.

Core vocabulary

meals	las comidas
mealtimes	las horas de las comidas
breakfast	el desayuno
elevenses	el tentempié de las once
lunch	el almuerzo / la comida
afternoon tea	la merienda
dinner	la cena
supper	la cena
the menu	la carta
starter	la entrada / el primer plato
soup	la sopa
fish	el pescado
main course	el plato principal
dessert	el postre
cheese	el queso
coffee	el café

- wine is drunk at many meals, but always balanced with mineral water
- Spanish people often eat with a fork in the right hand, and bread in the left hand
- mealtimes are a family occasion, to be enjoyed, and definitely not to be rushed

drinks	*las bebidas*
soft drink	el refresco
orange juice	el zumo / jugo de naranja
water	el agua
mineral water	el agua mineral
fizzy	con gas
still	sin gas
aperitif	el aperitivo
cocktail	el cóctel
sherry	el jerez
gin and tonic	el gin-tonic
red wine	el vino tinto
white wine	el vino blanco
champagne	el champán
brandy	el coñac
liqueur	el licor

Here are a few examples of popular Spanish dishes to give you a taster!

starters	*entradas*
cold meats	los fiambres
hors d'oeuvres	los entremeses
Spanish omelette	la tortilla española
macaroni with tomato sauce	los macarrones con tomate
Russian salad	la ensaladilla rusa

soups	*sopas*
noodle soup	la sopa de fideos
fish soup	la sopa de pescado
garlic soup	la sopa de ajo
consommé	el consomé
chilled vegetable soup	el gazpacho

stews	*cocidos*
chickpea stew	el cocido de garbanzos
lentil stew	el potaje de lentejas
Asturian bean stew	la fabada asturiana

fish and seafood
hake
tuna
sardines
squid
mussels

meat
steak
veal fillet
pork chop
roast chicken
stewed lamb

vegetables
green vegetables
peas
green beans
beans
cauliflower
aubergine
pepper
lettuce
tomato
cucumber
mixed salad
potatoes
chips / crisps
rice
pasta
spaghetti

desserts
frozen tart
fruit salad
yoghurt
caramel custard
peaches in syrup
cream
ice cream

flavours of ice cream
coconut
pistachio
strawberry
raspberry

pescados y mariscos
la merluza
el atún
las sardinas
los calamares
los mejillones

la carne
el bistec
el filete de ternera
la chuleta de cerdo
el pollo asado
el estofado de cordero

los vegetales
las verduras
los guisantes
las judías verdes
las habas
la coliflor
la berenjena
el pimiento
la lechuga
el tomate
el pepino
la ensalada mixta
las patatas
las patatas fritas
el arroz
las pastas
los espaguetis

los postres
la tarta helada
la macedonia de fruta
el yogur
el flan
el melocotón en almíbar
la nata
el helado

los sabores
el coco
el pistacho
la fresa
la frambuesa

vanilla	la vainilla
lemon	el limón
chocolate	el chocolate

coffee — ***el café***

espresso	el café esprés
cappuccino	el capuchino
coffee with milk	el café con leche
coffee without milk	el café solo
with sugar	con azúcar
with sweetener	con edulcorante
without sugar	sin azúcar
decaffeinated coffee	el café descafeinado

tea — ***el té***

Indian tea	el té indio
China tea	el té chino
herbal tea	la infusión de hierbas
fruit tea	la infusión de fruta
with milk	con leche
with lemon	con limón
with sugar	con azúcar

Useful phrases

I *have a special diet.*	Estoy a una dieta especial.
I *am allergic to …*	Soy alérgico/a a …
I *don't eat …*	No como …
I *can't eat …*	No puedo comer …
I *am a vegetarian.*	Soy vegetariano.
I *am a vegan.*	Soy vegetariano estricto.
I *have to have a gluten-free diet.*	Sigo una dieta sin gluten.
I *am diabetic.*	Soy diabético.

Useful verbs

to like / dislike	gustar*
to eat	comer
to drink	beber
to prefer	preferir
to love	amar

* Remember that **gustar** is special – it works back to front (see p. 57).

6.3 Breakfast

Core vocabulary

cereals	los cereales
wheat	el trigo
oats	la avena
barley	la cebada
rye	el centeno
bran	el salvado
cornflakes	los copos de maíz
muesli	el muesli
milk	la leche
semi-skimmed milk	la leche semi-desnatada
fat-free milk	la leche desnatada
soya milk	la leche de soja
goat's milk	la leche de cabra
cream	la nata
yoghurt	el yogur
bacon	el bacón
eggs	los huevos
scrambled	revueltos
poached	escalfado
boiled	pasados por agua
hard boiled	duro
fried	fritos
sunny side up	frito sólo por un lado
sausages	las salchichas
hash browns	croquetas de patata y cebolla
mushrooms	los champiñones
tomatoes	los tomates
fried	fritos
grilled	a la parrilla
tinned	en lata
baked beans	judías en salsa de tomate
pancake	la tortita
maple syrup	el jarabe de arce
ham	el jamón
salami	el salami
cheese	el queso
bread	el pan
white	blanco
brown	moreno

granary	con granos enteros
wholemeal	integral
sliced	en rebanadas
organic	orgánico
rolls	los panecillos
croissants	los croissants
danish pastries	los bollos de hojaldre daneses
butter	la mantequilla
margarine	la margarina
low-fat spread	la margarina con poca materia grasa
jam	la mermelada
marmalade	la mermelada de naranja
honey	la miel
peanut butter	la mantequilla de cacahuete
drinks	las bebidas
tea	el té
coffee	el café
milk	la leche
cold milk	la leche fría
hot milk	la leche caliente
hot chocolate	el chocolate caliente
fruit juice	el zumo de fruta
orange juice	el zumo de naranja
freshly squeezed orange juice	el zumo de naranja recién exprimido

Useful phrases

I don't eat breakfast.	No tomo el desayuno.
I only eat …	Sólo como …
I don't drink milk …	No bebo (la) leche …
I have my breakfast at …	Desayuno a las …

6.4 Snacks

Core vocabulary

snack	el tentempié
a (ham)burger	una hamburguesa
cheeseburger	una hamburguesa con queso
fishburger	una hamburguesa de pescado
salad	una ensalada
green salad	una ensalada verde

tomato salad	una ensalada con tomate
mixed salad	una ensalada mixta
potato salad	una ensaladilla de patatas
Russian salad	una ensaladilla rusa
yoghurt	el yogur
biscuit / cookie	la galleta
chocolate biscuit	la galleta de chocolate
piece of cake	el trozo de pastel
bun	el bollo
sweets	los caramelos
sandwich (English style)	el sándwich
in brown bread	en pan moreno
in white bread	en pan blanco
in a roll	en un panecillo
sandwich (Spanish style)	el bocadillo
with mayonnaise / salad dressing	con mayonesa / aliño
without mayonnaise / salad dressing	sin mayonesa / aliño

Useful phrases

Can I offer you a cup of coffee?	¿Te apetece un café?
How do you take it?	¿Cómo lo prefieres?
With milk or without milk?	¿Con leche o sin leche?
Do you take sugar?	¿Lo tomas con azúcar?
Have you got a sweetener?	¿Tienes un edulcorante?
Would you like a biscuit?	¿Te gustaría una galleta?
Yes please.	Sí, por favor.
No thank you.	No, gracias.
I am on a diet.	Estoy a dieta.
I don't take ...	No tomo / como / bebo ...
It's too hot / cold / spicy.	Es demasiado caliente / frío / picante.
It isn't cooked properly.	No está bien guisado.
It is delicious!	Es / está muy delicioso / rico.

6.5 Fruit and vegetables

Useful vocabulary

fruit   ***la fruta***

   apple   la manzana
   cooking apple   la manzana para cocer
   dessert apple   la manzana para repostería
   apricot   el albaricoque
   banana   el plátano
   grapes   las uvas
   cherries   las cerezas
   melon   el melón
   watermelon   la sandía
   peach   el melocotón
   pear   la pera
   plum   la ciruela
   raspberry   la frambuesa
   rhubarb   el ruibarbo
   strawberry   la fresa

salad   ***la ensalada***

   cucumber   el pepino
   lettuce   la lechuga
   olives   las aceitunas
   radish   el rábano
   spring onion   la cebolleta
   tomatoes   los tomates

vegetables   ***las legumbres / los vegetales / las verduras***

   beans   las habas
   green beans   las judías verdes
   broccoli   el brécol
   cabbage   la col
   carrot   la zanahoria
   cauliflower   la coliflor
   aubergine   la berenjena
   courgette   el calabacín
   pepper   el pimiento
   garlic   el ajo
   leek   el puerro
   lettuce   la lechuga

mushroom	el champiñón
onion	la cebolla
potato	la patata
sweetcorn	el maíz
turnip	el nabo
swede	el nabo sueco
pumpkin	la calabaza
shallots	los chalotes
spinach	las espinacas
watercress	el berro

citrus fruits — *las frutas cítricas*

grapefruit	el pomelo
lemon	el limón
lime	la lima
orange	la naranja

berries — *las bayas*

blackberry	la mora
blueberry / bilberry / cranberry	el arándano
gooseberry	la grosella
blackcurrant	la grosella negra
redcurrant	la grosella roja

exotic fruits — *las frutas exóticas*

avocado	el aguacate
coconut	el coco
date	el dátil
fig	el higo
kiwi fruit	el kiwi
mango	el mango
passion fruit	la granadilla
pineapple	la piña

nuts — *las nueces*

almond	la almendra
brazil	la nuez del Brasil
cashew	el anacardo
hazel	la avellana
peanut	el cacahuete
pistachio	el pistacho
walnut	la nuez

pulses — *las leguminosas*

| beans | las habas |
| chillibeans | los frijoles |

lentils	las lentejas
chickpeas	los garbanzos

6.6 Fish and meat

seafood	***los mariscos***
fish*	el pez, el pescado
anchovy	las anchoas
cod	el bacalao
eel	la anguila
haddock	el eglefino
hake	la merluza
herring	el arenque
jellyfish	la medusa
mackerel	la caballa
octopus	el pulpo
plaice	la platija
red mullet	el salmonete
sardine	la sardina
sea bass	el besugo
skate	la raya
sole	el lenguado
squid	el calamar
tuna	el atún
whiting	la pescadilla

shellfish	***los mariscos***
crab	el cangrejo
langoustine	el langostino
lobster	la langosta
mussels	los mejillones
oyster	la ostra
prawn	la gamba

fresh water fish	***el pez de agua fresca***
trout	la trucha
salmon	el salmón
perch	la perca
pike	el lucio

*NB there are two words for fish: **el pez** – live fish, and **el pescado** – 'fished' fish, ready to buy / cook / eat!

meat	**la carne**
beef	la vaca
lamb	el cordero
pork	el cerdo
veal	la ternera
ham	el jamón
liver	el hígado
kidneys	los riñones
(cooked) sausage	el embutido
hard, spicy pork sausage	el chorizo
black pudding	la morcilla
long pork sausage	la longaniza
tripe	los callos

poultry	**las aves**
chicken	el pollo
turkey	el pavo
duck	el pato
goose	el ganso

game	**la caza**
grouse	el urogallo
hare	la liebre
partridge	la perdiz
pheasant	el faisán
pigeon	el pichón
rabbit	el conejo
venison	la carne de venado
wild boar	el jabalí

6.7 Using a recipe

Core vocabulary

making a cake	hacer un pastel
ingredients	los ingredientes
flour	la harina
plain flour	la harina sin levadura
self-raising flour	la harina con levadura
raising agent (baking powder)	la levadura en polvo
cornflour	la harina de maíz
potato flower	la harina de patata

sugar	el azúcar
butter	la mantequilla
salt	la sal
vanilla / almond essence	la esencia de vainilla / almendra
grated chocolate	el chocolate rallado
melted chocolate	el chocolate fundido
grated lemon rind	la ralladura de limón
the juice of an orange	el zumo de una naranja
chopped nuts	las nueces picadas
weighing scales	la balanza
mixing bowl	el cuenco grande
wooden spoon	la cuchara de palo
mixer	la batidora
grater	el rallador
sieve	el colador / la criba
baking tin	el molde (para el horno)
oven	el horno
oven gloves	los guantes para el horno
saucepan	la cacerola
casserole	la cacerola / cazuela
frying pan	la sartén
lid	la tapa
handle	la manga
silver foil	el papel de aluminio
cling film	el film adhesivo
grease-proof paper	el papel encerado
plastic bags	las bolsas de plástico
plastic containers	las recipientes de plástico

Useful phrases

make a cake	hacer un pastel
make soup	hacer la sopa
prepare the vegetables	preparar las verduras
peel the carrots	pelar las zanahorias
chop the leeks	picar los puerros
melt the butter	fundir la mantequilla
add the flour	añadir la harina
stir the mixture	agitar la mezcla
pour in the stock	echar / verter el caldo

Useful verbs

heat	calentar
cook	cocinar
roast	asar
bake	cocer
fry	freír
boil	hervir
poach (egg)	escalfar
poach (fish)	hervir
steam	cocer al vapor

07

in the town

7.1 The town plan and the sights

Core vocabulary

about the town	*en la ciudad*
bank	el banco
bus station	la estación de autobuses
car park	el aparcamiento / estacionamiento
cinema	el cine
council offices	las oficinas municipales
football ground	el estadio / campo de fútbol
hospital	el hospital
hotel	el hotel
law courts	los tribunales de justicia
library	la biblioteca
market	el mercado
museum	el museo
police station	la comisaría
post office	(la oficina de) Correos
station	la estación
swimming pool	la piscina
tourist office	la oficina de (información y) turismo
town hall	el ayuntamiento
region	la región
district	el distrito
built-up area	la zona urbanizada
town	el pueblo
suburbs	los suburbios
town centre	el centro de la ciudad
industrial zone	la zona industrial
opening times	las horas de apertura
open	abierto/a
closed	cerrado/a
holidays	las vacaciones
bank holiday	el día festivo
annual holiday	la fiesta anual

the sights	*los lugares de interés*
bridge	el puente
castle	el castillo
cathedral	la catedral
church	la iglesia

fountain	la fuente
monument	el monumento
museum	el museo
old town	el casco viejo
opera house	el teatro de la ópera
park	el parque
river	el río
square	la plaza
statue	la estatua
theatre	el teatro

Useful verbs

to meet	reunirse / encontrar
to look for	buscar
to be situated	estar situado/a

Useful phrases

Let's meet at the café Goya.	Nos quedamos en el café Goya
Where is it...?	¿Dónde está ...?
It is in the centre.	Está en el centro.
on the main street.	en la calle principal.
near the post office.	cerca de Correos.
opposite the bank.	enfrente del banco.
on the market place.	en la plaza del mercado.
beside the river.	a orillas del río.

7.2 Getting around town

Core vocabulary

road	la carretera (*between towns*)
road / street	la calle (*in towns*)
avenue	la avenida
pavement	la acera
gutter	la cuneta
pedestrian crossing	el paso de peatones
pedestrian zone	la zona peatonal
traffic lights	el semáforo
crossing lights	las luces del paso de peatones
subway (foot passage)	el paso subterráneo

the bus stop	la parada de autobuses
the subway / tube station	la estación de metro

How do I get into town?
¿Por dónde / cómo puedo ir a la ciudad?

by car	en coche
by bus	en autobús
by tram	en tranvía
by subway (metro)	en metro

parking the car
aparcar el coche

car park	el aparcamiento
multistorey car park	el aparcamiento de varias plantas
underground car park	el parking subterráneo
full	completo
spaces	espacios (libres)
entrance	la entrada
ticket machine	la máquina de billetes
change	el cambio / suelto
credit card	la carta de crédito
ticket	el billete / la entrada
exit	la salida
barrier	la barrera
traffic warden	el guardia de tráfico

Useful phrases

Use the crossing.	Usar el paso de peatones.
Don't cross.	No cruce.
There's a car coming.	Llega un coche.
Excuse me ...	Diga(me) / Oiga(me)
Can you tell me ...?	¿Me puede decir ...?
How do I get to the station	¿Por dónde se va a la estación?
Where is the nearest car park?	¿Dónde está el aparcamiento más cercano?
When is the next bus?	¿A qué hora pasa el próximo autobús?
It is forbidden ... to cross the road here.	Prohibido ... cruzar la calle aquí.
to drop litter.	dejar caer basura/papeles.
to park.	aparcar.

Useful verbs

to *walk*	andar / ir andando
to *cross*	cruzar
to *turn left / right*	girar a / tomar la derecha / izquierda
to *go straight on*	seguir todo recto / derecho
to *run*	correr
to *drive*	llevar el coche a ...
to *catch the bus*	coger el autobús
to *miss the bus*	perder el autobús

7.3 Shops and shopping

Core vocabulary

shops	*las tiendas*
bakery	la panadería
butcher	la carnicería
cake shop	la pastelería
chemist's	la farmacia
clothes shop	la boutique / la tienda de ropa
confectioner's	la confitería
department store	el almacén / los almacenes
dry-cleaner's	la tintorería
flower shop	la floristería
hairdresser	el peluquero
health food store	la tienda de alimentos dietéticos
hypermarket	el hipermercado
market	el mercado
newsagent's	el tienda de periódicos
optician	la óptica
shoe shop	la zapatería
shopping centre	el centro comercial
sports shop	la tienda de deportes
supermarket	el supermercado
travel agent	la agencia de viajes

store guide	*la guía del almacén*
escalator	la escalera mecánica
lift	el ascensor
ground floor	la planta baja

first floor	el primer piso
bedding	la ropa de cama
fashion	la moda
sportswear	la ropa deportiva
casual wear	la ropa de sport / ropa informal
leather goods	los artículos de cuero
television and electrical goods	la tienda de televisión y electrodomésticos
sales person	el dependiente / la dependienta
cash desk	la caja
changing room	el vestuario
customer, client	el cliente
price	el precio
deposit	el depósito
discount	el descuento
reductions / sales	rebajas
reduced prices	precios reducidos
clearance / closing-down sale	liquidación
bargain offers	ofertas
bargains	gangas

Useful phrases

How much does it cost?	¿Cuánto cuesta?
How are you paying?	¿Cómo va a pagar?
Are you paying cash?	¿Paga al contado?
Do you have the right change?	¿Tiene la vuelta correcta?
Will you wrap it as a gift?	¿Lo puede envolver en papel de regalo?
out of stock	agotado

Useful verbs

to buy	comprar
to sell	vender
to look for	buscar
to pay	pagar
to prefer	preferir
to go shopping	ir de compras
to order	pedir / encargar
to deliver	entregar
to window shop	mirar escaparates

7.4 At the supermarket

Core vocabulary

food department	la sección de comestibles
fruit and vegetables	fruta y verduras
dairy products	productos lácteos
frozen foods	productos congelados
cleaning materials	productos de limpieza
electrical goods	electrodomésticos
household appliances	electrodomésticos
wines and spirits	vinos y licores
drinks	bebidas
photographic shop	la tienda de material fotográfico
dry-cleaning	la tintorería
flower shop	la floristería
card shop	la tienda de tarjetas
shopping list	la lista de compras
assistant	el dependiente
basket	la cesta
trolley	el carrito
cash machine	el cajero automático
check out	la caja

Useful verbs

to weigh	pesar
to look for	buscar
to find	encontrar
to deliver	entregar

Useful phrases

Where is / are the … ?	¿Dónde está(n) …?
on the …. aisle	en el pasillo …
on the shelf	en el estante …
on the row with the …	en el pasillo con el / la …
at the far end	al otro extremo
on the left / right-hand side	a mano derecha / izquierda
What time do you shut?	¿A qué hora cierra(n)?
Are you open on a Sunday?	¿Abren los domingos?

7.5 At the post office and the bank

Core vocabulary

letter box	el buzón
post (letters and parcels in general)	Correos
letter	la carta
packet	el paquete
parcel	el paquete
postcard	la (tarjeta) postal
writing paper	el papel de escribir
envelope	el sobre
pen	la pluma
biro / ballpoint	el bolígrafo
form	el formulario / impreso
stamp	el sello
postman	el cartero
phone card	la tarjeta telefónica
printed matter	impresos
recorded delivery	el servicio de entrega con acuse de recibo
overnight delivery	la entrega / el reparto de la noche a la mañana
air mail	(correo) por avión
money	el dinero
cash	el (dinero en) efectivo
coins	las monedas
notes	los billetes (de banco)
cheque book	el talonario (de cheques)
credit card	la tarjeta de crédito
cash machine	el cajero automático
a cash transfer	una transferencia bancaria
the date	la fecha
the amount	la cantidad
signature	la firma
the bank code	el número de agencia del banco
the credit card number	el número de carta de crédito
the expiry date	la fecha de vencimiento
balance	el saldo
loan	el préstamo
mortgage	la hipoteca

Useful phrases

insert your card	introducir la tarjeta
type in your number	teclee su número
wait	espere
remove your card	saque su carta
take your money	coja su dinero
fill in the form	rellene el formulario
go to the counter / cash desk	vaya a la caja
Where do I have to sign?	¿Dónde tengo que firmar?
How much does it cost to send this to …?	¿Cuánto cuesta / vale para mandar esto a...?
By air mail	por avión

Useful verbs

to cash	cobrar
to deposit	ingresar
to transfer	transferir
to sign	firmar
to fill in	rellenar

08

in the country

- Spain occupies most of the Iberian Peninsula, with Portugal taking up the remainder. It is situated in a strategically important position at the mouth of the Mediterranean, and bridges the closest point between Africa and Europe.

- Spain is a high tableland – it has an average height second only to Switzerland in Europe – tilted in such a way that much of the highest land is in the north and east, and the lowest in the south and west; several high but flattish areas are known as *meseta*. This is criss-crossed by mountain ranges – *sierras* – and rivers, mainly orientated from east to west.

- In its geography and climate, Spain is a land of great variety and contrasts: the north and north-west have a wet, moderate Atlantic climate; the centre has a continental climate – extremes of very hot, dry summers and very cold winters; the east and south-east have a Mediterranean climate – mild, wet winters and hot, dry summers; the far south also has a Mediterranean climate, but with warmer winters and higher temperatures overall. All of this is varied by local micro-climates, principally because of the many mountain ranges: even the mountains in the far south – the Sierra Nevada – are snow-capped for much of the year (hence the name!)

- Spain used to be a largely agricultural country, and several crops are still very important, notably production of olive oil (Spain is the world's greatest producer), wine, fruit and vegetables. Much of its territory, however, is wild or semi-wild, being so mountainous; large areas are covered with forest, and some lower areas are so dry as to be almost desert-like except where irrigation enables agricultural activity.

- In the 20th century, Spain developed industry, notably in the north and north-east; after the Spanish Civil War of 1936–9, the growth of mass tourism helped to fund a tremendous economic recovery which pulled Spain back into line with the other main countries of western Europe; this in its turn facilitated Spain's membership of the European Union and involvement in NATO. Spain is now one of the most visited countries in the world, known for its pleasant climate and quality of life.

8.1 The countryside

Core vocabulary

in the countryside	*en el campo*
field	el campo
meadow	el prado
footpath	el sendero
hill	la colina
mountain	la montaña
stream	el arroyo
river	el río
lake	el lago
valley	el valle
grass	la hierba
plant	la planta
wild flower	la flor silvestre
moss	el musgo
fungi	los hongos
fern	el helecho
bush	el arbusto
tree	el árbol
wood	el bosque
forest	la selva
hedge	el seto
fence	la valla
ditch	la zanja
gate	la verja
spring	la fuente / el manantial
pond	el charco / estanque
bridge	el puente
waterfall	la cascada
weir	la presa / encañizada
watermill	el molino de agua
reservoir	el embalse
dam	la presa
flood	la inundación
copse	el bosquecillo
beech	la haya
chestnut	el castaño
elm	el olmo
oak	el roble

| sycamore | el sicomoro |
| willow | el sauce |

Useful verbs

to go for a walk	dar un paseo / ir de paseo / pasearse
to go swimming	bañarse (nadar = to swim)
to go hiking	ir de excursión a pie
to ride a bike	montar en bicicleta
to go fishing	ir de pesca
to flood (a river)	desbordarse

8.2 In the mountains

Core vocabulary

hill	la colina
mountain	la montaña
mountain range	la sierra
mountain pass	el puerto
mountain path	el sendero de montaña
mountain railway	el funicular / ferrocarril de montaña
mountain hut / refuge	el albergue de montaña
cable car	el teleférico
summit	la cumbre
the weather	el tiempo
cloudy	nuboso
rainy	lluvioso
sunny	soleado
dry	seco
windy	de mucho viento / ventoso
easy	fácil
moderate difficulty	dificultad moderada
difficult	difícil
extreme	dificultad extrema
peak	el pico
rock face	la pared de roca
slope	la vertiente
gorge	el cañón / barranco
cave	la cueva

equipment	el equipo / las herramientas
rope	la cuerda
harness	el arnés
carabiner	el mosquetón
rucksack	la mochila
torch	la linterna
stove	la cocina/estufa
dried food	los alimentos secos
waterproofs	los impermeables
pen knife	la navaja
water bottle	la cantimplora
sleeping bag	el saco de dormir
tent	la tienda de campaña

Useful phrases

What is the forecast?	¿Cuál es el pronóstico del tiempo?
How difficult is it?	¿Qué nivel de dificultad tiene?
How long does it take?	¿Cuánto tiempo hace falta para hacerlo?

Useful verbs

to climb	escalar
to abseil	hacer rappel
to bivouac	vivaquear
to hike	ir de excursión a pie / dar una caminata
to rock climb	escalar en rocas
to boulder	escalar en cantos rodados
to ice climb	escalar en hielo

8.3 At the seaside

Core vocabulary

seaside	la playa / la orilla del mar
sea	el mar
ocean	el océano
wave	la ola

harbour	el puerto
port	el puerto
jetty	el muelle / embarcadero
pier	el embarcadero / muelle
quay	el muelle
beach	la playa
sand	la arena
sand dune	la duna
cliff	el acantilado / risco
shell	la concha
pebbles	los guijarros
rock	la roca
island	la isla
reef	el arrecife
surf	las olas rompientes
shore	la orilla
estuary	el estuario
cape	el cabo
promontory	el promontorio
peninsula	la península
boat	el barco
rowing boat	la barca de remos / el bote de remo
yacht	el velero / barco de vela
sailing dinghy	el bote
rubber dinghy	la lancha neumática
motor boat	la lancha motora
ferry	la barca (de pasaje)
car ferry	el ferry / transbordador
cruiser	el crucero
liner	el transatlántico
pilot (harbour)	el práctico
sailing	la vela / navegación a vela
navigation	la navegación
port	babor
starboard	estribor
buoy	la boya
lighthouse	el faro
mast	el mástil
sail	la vela
rudder	el timón
anchor	el ancla (f)
satellite positioning	el posicionamiento / la ubicación por satélite

automatic pilot	el piloto automático
ropes	los cabos
high tide	la marea alta
low tide	la marea baja
sea level	el nivel del mar
calm	en calma / tranquilo
choppy	agitado
rough	agitado / encrespado
sandy	arenoso
rocky	rocoso
rough	desigual
smooth	liso

Useful phrases

When is high tide?	¿cuándo llega la marea alta?
Where can I moor?	¿dónde puedo amarrar / atracar?

Useful verbs

to row	remar
to sail	navegar (a vela)
to motor	navegar a motor
to cast off	soltar las amarras
to tie up	amarrar

8.4 Working in the country

Core vocabulary

agriculture	la agricultura
bee keeping	la apicultura
game keeping	el oficio del guardabosques
horticulture	la horticultura
wine growing	la vinicultura
forestry	la silvicultura
farm	la granja
market garden	el huerto / la huerta
farmhouse	el caserío

barn	el granero
stables	la cuadra
cattle shed	el establo
cattle	el ganado
cow / heifer / bull / calf	las vaca / la vaquilla / el toro / el ternero
sheep or ewe / ram / lamb	la oveja / el carnero / el cordero
pig or boar / sow / piglet	el cerdo / la puerca / el cerdito or lechón
(billy)goat / nanny / kid	el chivo or macho cabrío / la cabra / el cabrito
poultry	las aves (de corral)
chickens / hens	las gallinas / el pollo
duck / drake / ducklings	la pata / el pato / los patitos
goose / goslings	el ganso / los ansarinos
turkey	el pavo
pheasant	el faisán
sheep dog	el perro pastor
guard dog	el perro guardián
dog / bitch / puppy	el perro / la perra / el cachorro or perrito

crops
los cultivos / productos agrícolas

cereals	los cereales
grain	el grano
barley	la cebada
oats	la avena
rice	el arroz
rye	el centeno
wheat	el trigo
hay	el heno
straw	la paja
bee keeper	el apicultor
farmer	el granjero
farm worker	el jornalero / obrero agrícola
horticulturist	el horticultor
vet	el veterinario
wine grower	el viñador
vineyard	el viñedo
vines	las viñas

grapes	las uvas
fruit growing	la fruticultura
olives	las aceitunas
cultivating	el cultivo
planting	la plantación
spreading fertilizer	la fertilización / distribución de abonos
weeding	desherbar
harvesting	la cosecha
packaging	el embalaje / envasado
farm equipment	las herramientas agrícolas
tractor	el tractor
trailer	el remolque
plough	el arado
(combine) harvester	la cosechadora

Useful phrases

Beware of the dog / bull!	¡Cuidado al perro / toro!
Please shut the gate.	Por favor, cierre la barrera.
electric fence	la valla electrificada
No entry.	Se prohíbe la entrada.

Useful verbs

to feed	dar de comer a
to milk	ordeñar
to breed	criar
to sow	sembrar
to fertilize	abonar / fertilizar
to weed	desherbar
to pick	(re)coger / cosechar
to harvest	cosechar
to take to market	llevar al mercado

09

hobbies and sports

9.1 Hobbies

Core vocabulary

hobbies	*los pasatiempos*
acting	la interpretación
archaeology	la arqueología
astronomy	la astronomía
cooking	cocinar
dancing	bailar
modern	hacer baile moderno
ballroom	hacer el baile de salón
DIY	el bricolaje
drawing	dibujar
gardening	trabajar en el jardín
going out (socially)	salir (con amigos)
history	la historia
listening to music	escuchar música
meeting people	conocer a gente
painting	pintar
photography	la fotografía / sacar fotos
pottery	hacer cerámica
reading	leer / la lectura
sailing	hacer vela
sewing	coser / hacer costura
singing	cantar
sport	el deporte / hacer deporte
visiting historical sites	visitar sitios históricos
watching films	ver películas
watching television	ver la tele(visión)
writing	escribir

outdoor pursuits	*actividades al aire libre*
birdwatching	observar aves
fishing	pescar / la pesca
horse riding	montar a caballo
hunting	cazar / la caza
rambling	el excursionismo a pie
shooting	(hacer) el tiro
walking	pasearse / dar paseos

indoor games	
chess	el ajedrez
cards	los naipes
bridge	el bridge
party games	juegos de fiesta

happy families	el juego de las familias
bingo	el bingo
jigsaw puzzles	puzzles / rompecabezas
dominoes	el dominó
draughts	las damas
billards	el billar
snooker	el snooker
table football	el futbolín
cross word	la crucigrama

music	***la música***
making music	tocar música
playing in an orchestra	tocar en una orquesta
singing in a group	cantar en un grupo
playing an instrument	tocar un instrumento
piano	el piano
guitar	la guitarra
violin	el violín
trumpet	la trompeta
drums	la batería

Useful verbs

to attend	asistir a
to be a member of ...	ser socio / miembro de ...
to be interested in ...	tener interés en ...
(I am interested in ...)	me interesa ...
to be keen on	ser aficionado/a a
to enjoy	gustar (me gusta ... I enjoy ...)
to meet	encontrar / conocer (to get to know)
to spend my time	pasar el tiempo
to play	jugar a

Useful phrases

What do you do in your free time?	¿Qué hace(s) en tu tiempo libre?
Do you like ...?	¿Te / le gusta ...?
I like meeting people.	Me gusta conocer a gente.
I do (painting).	Pinto / Hago pintura.
I belong to a club.	Soy socio de un club.
We meet every ...	Nos reunimos cada ...
It's interesting.	Es interesante.
It's fantastic.	Es fantástico.
It's boring.	Es aburrido.

9.2 Sports

ball games	los juegos de pelota / balón
football	el fútbol
footballer	el futbolista
ball	el balón
team	el equipo
goal	el gol
match	el partido
football ground	el campo de fútbol / el estadio (*stadium*)
score	el tanto
rugby	el rugby
player	el jugador
pitch	el campo de rugby
to score a try	marcar un ensayo
basketball	el baloncesto
basket	la canasta
volleyball	el voleibol
net	la red
handball	el balonmano
hockey	el hockey
hockey stick	el palo de hockey
golf	el golf
golf club	el palo de golf
golf course	el campo de golf
green	el green
hole	el hoyo
bunker	el búnker

Note that the vast majority of sports are masculine.

racket sports	*juegos de raqueta*
tennis	el tenis
tennis racquet	la raqueta de tenis
tennis court	la pista de tenis
tennis ball	la pelota de tenis
tennis player	el jugador de tenis / tenista
badminton	el bádminton
net	la red
shuttlecock	el volante
squash	el squash
squash court	la cancha de squash
squash racquet	la raqueta de squash

martial arts	***las artes marciales***
judo	el judo
karate	el karate
taekwando	el tae-kwondo
wrestling	la lucha libre

athletics	***el atletismo***
running	correr
cross country	el cross
jumping	(las pruebas de) salto
hurdles	las vallas
track	la pista

keep fit	***la gimnasia (para mantenerse en forma)***
aerobics	el aeróbic(o)
gymnastics	la gimnasia
jogging	el footing / jogging
weightlifting	el levantamiento de pesas
weight training	el entrenamiento con pesos
yoga	el yoga

Useful verbs

to win	ganar
to lose	perder
to draw	empatar
to box	boxear
to do	hacer
to jog	hacer footing
to run	correr

Contrary to popular belief, football is the national sport in Spain (bullfighting is a festival – **la fiesta nacional**). Basketball, handball and cycling are other popular sports for participants and spectators. In the Basque country **pelota** is played in every district and village – this is a sort of very fast, outdoor racket game with some general similarities to squash. Spain's climate favours outdoor games such as golf, tennis, and many Spaniards enjoy skiing in the snow-covered mountain areas, as well as swimming, water sports and other outdoor activities. Village squares and parks are often the venue for **petanca,** a Spanish version of **boules.**

9.3 More sports

water sports	***los deportes acuáticos***
canoeing	el piragüismo
canoe	la piragua
paddle	la pala
diving (deep sea)	el buceo (de altura)
wet suit	el traje isotérmico
dry suit	el traje seco
gas bottles	los tanques de gas
mask	la mascarilla
flippers	las aletas
snorkel	el tubo de respiración
rowing	el remo
boat	el barco
oars	los remos
sailing	la vela
sail	la vela
surfing	el surf
surf board	la plancha de surf
windsurfing	el windsurf
windsurfer	el surfista
yachting	la navegación a vela
yacht	el velero
dinghy	el bote
swimming	la natación
breast stroke	la braza de pecho
front crawl	el crol
butterfly	la braza de mariposa
backstroke	la espalda
diving	el salto de trampolín
swimming pool	la piscina
length	el largo
diving board	el trampolín
swimming costume	el traje de baño
goggles	los anteojos / las gafas de submarinismo
archery	el tiro con arco
bow	el arco
arrow	la flecha
target	el blanco / la diana
boxing	el boxeo
cycling	el ciclismo
racing bike	la bicicleta de carreras

mountain bike	la bicicleta de montaña
bike	la bicicleta
handlebars	los manillares
saddle	la silla
fencing	la esgrima
foil	el florete
horse riding	la equitación
saddle	la silla de montar
bridle	la brida / el freno
stirrups	el estribo
roller skating	el patinaje sobre ruedas
skates	los patines
skateboarding	el monopatinaje
skateboard	el monopatín
climbing	el montañismo
mountaineering	el alpinismo
rock climbing	la escalada en rocas
pot holing / caving	la espeleología
climbing boots	las botas de montañismo
rope	la cuerda
carabiner	el mosquetón
rucksack	la mochila
skiing	el esquí
skis	los esquís
poles	los bastones
piste	la pista
snowboarding, snowboard	el snowboard
sledging, sledge	el trineo
tobogganing, toboggan	el tobogán
ice skating	el patinaje sobre hielo
skates	los patines
ice rink	la pista de patinaje sobre hielo

Useful phrases

I enjoy doing …	Me encanta …
I am good at …	Soy fuerte en …
I am not good at …	No soy fuerte en …

10

clothing

10.1 Garments and styles

Core vocabulary

ladies' fashion   *la moda femenina*
  blouse   la blusa
  cardigan   la rebeca / chaqueta de punto
  clothes   los vestidos / la ropa
  dress   el vestido
    evening dress   el traje de noche
    sundress   el vestido de playa
  jacket   la chaqueta
    long jacket   la chaqueta larga
    short jacket   la chaqueta corta
  jersey   el jersey / el suéter
  shorts   el short / pantalón corto
  skirt   la falda
  suit   el traje
  trouser suit   el traje pantalón
  trousers   el pantalón

  lingerie   la ropa interior femenina
  bra   el sostén / sujetador
  knickers   las braguitas
  slip   la enagua / combinación
  stockings   las medias
  tights   los pantis

  nightie   el camisón de noche
  pyjamas   el pijama
  negligee   el negligé / salto de cama

men's fashion   *la moda masculina*
  blazer   la chaqueta de sport / blazer
  dinner jacket   el esmoquin / smóking
  jacket   la chaqueta / americana
  jeans   los vaqueros / tejanos /
                  bluejeans
  jumper   el jersey / el suéter
  pullover   el jersey / el suéter
  shirt   la camisa
  shorts   el short / el pantalón corto
  socks   los calcetines
  suit   el traje

sweatshirt	la sudadera
T-shirt	la camiseta
tie	la corbata
trousers	el pantalón
belt	el cinturón
braces	los tirantes
waistcoat	el chaleco
boxers	los calzones
shorts	el short / los calzones
vest	la camiseta
pyjamas	el pijama
coat	el abrigo
raincoat	el impermeable
jacket	la chaqueta
hat	el sombrero
scarf	la bufanda
gloves	los guantes

Useful verbs

to wear	llevar (puesto)
to fit	quedar bien
to suit	quedar bien / sentar bien

Useful phrases

Does it fit / suit me?	¿Me queda bien? / ¿Me sienta bien?
I will be wearing …	Llevaré puesto …
a dark suit.	un traje oscuro.
a coat and hat.	un sombrero y un abrigo.
a sweatshirt, jeans and trainers.	una sudadera, vaqueros y zapatillas
What will you be wearing?	¿Qué llevará(s) puesto?
What size are you?	¿Qué talla tiene(s) / usa(s)?
It is too short (for me).	Es demasiado corto / me queda corto.
It is too short.	Es demasiado corto / le queda corto.
too wide	demasiado ancho
too long	demasiado largo
too tight	demasiado estrecho
Have you got anything bigger / smaller?	¿Tiene(s) algo más grande / pequeño?
in a different colour?	en otro color?

It suits you / it doesn't suit you.	(No) Te / le queda bien.
They suit you / they don't suit you.	(No) Te / le quedan bien.
menswear department	la sección de moda masculina
ladieswear department	la sección de moda femenina
childrenswear department	la sección de moda juvenil

Useful verbs

Many verbs to do with clothing are reflexive verbs (see pp. 18–19)

to get dressed	vestirse
I get dressed	me visto
to get undressed	desnudarse
I get undressed	me desnudo
to put on one's shirt	ponerse al camisa
I put on my shirt	me pongo la camisa
to take off one's shirt	quitarse la camisa
I take off my shirt	me quito la camisa

10.2 The garment

measurements	las medidas
tape measure	la cinta métrica
length	el largo
width	el ancho
size	la talla
collar	el collar
neck	el cuello
shoulders	los hombros
sleeves	las mangas
chest	el pecho
waist	la cintura
cuffs	los puños
hips	(la talla de) cadera
inside leg	(la medida de) la entrepierna
materials	las telas / los tejidos
fabric	la tela / el tejido
cotton	el algodón
fur	la piel
artificial fur	la piel artificial
jersey	el tejido de punto
leather	la piel / el cuero

linen	el lino
satin	el satén / raso
silk	la seda
suede	el ante
synthetic fibre	la fibra sintética
tweed	el tweed
velvet	el terciopelo
wool	la lana
floral	de flores / floreado
multi-colour	multicolor
patterned	estampado
pleated	con tablas / plisado
plain (one colour)	de un solo color
self colour	de color uniforme / unicolor
spotted	de lunares
striped	a rayas
button	el botón
fastener	el corchete
needle	la aguja
ribbon	la cinta
scissors	las tijeras
sewing machine	la máquina de coser
thread	el algodón
velcro	el velcro
zip	la cremallera
detergent	el detergente
detergent for wool	el detergente para lana
fabric softener	el suavizante
soap powder	el detergente en polvo

Useful verbs

to wash	lavar
to dry	secar
to dry-clean	lavar en seco
to iron	planchar
to mend	remendar
to darn	zurcir

Useful phrases

| I have lost a button. | Se me ha caído un botón. |
| Can I get this laundered / dry-cleaned / pressed (ironed)? | ¿Puedo hacer lavar / lavar en seco / planchar esto? |

How long will it take?	¿Cuánto tiempo hace falta para hacerlo?
Can you remove this stain?	¿Puede(s) quitar esta mancha?
Can you sew this button on?	¿Puede(s) coser este botón?
Can you take it in?	¿Puede(s) achicarlo/la?
Can you shorten it?	¿Puede(s) acortarlo/la?
This garment must be dry-cleaned.	Esta prenda tiene que lavarse en seco.
This garment can be machine washed.	Esta prenda puede lavarse a máquina.
Hand-wash only.	Esta prenda sólo se debe lavar a mano.
Don't use bleach.	No use(s) lejía.
made in …	confeccionado en …

10.3 Special occasions

Core vocabulary

going to work   *al trabajo*
- *uniform*   el uniforme
- *apron*   el delantal
- *overall*   el mono

it's raining   *llueve / está lloviendo*
- *rain coat*   el impermeable
- *rain hat*   el sombrero impermeable
- *rubber boots*   las botas de agua / goma
- *umbrella*   el paraguas
- *waterproof trousers*   el pantalón impermeable

it's cold   *hace frío*
- *anorak*   el ánorak
- *gloves*   los guantes
- *thick socks*   los calcetines gruesos
- *woolly hat*   el sombrero de lana

on the beach   *en la playa*
- *bikini*   el bikini
- *flip flops*   las chancletas
- *flippers*   las aletas
- *goggles*   las gafas de bucear / gafas submarinas

snorkel	el esnórquel
suntan cream	el bronceador
swimming costume	el traje de baño
trunks	el bañador

to spend a night on the town *salir de juerga*

casual dress	la ropa informal
evening dress	el traje de noche (*women*)
	traje de etiqueta (*men*)
formal dress	la ropa de etiqueta
high heels	los tacones altos
smart clothes	la ropa elegante

playing the game *jugando a los deportes*

baseball hat	el sombrero de béisbol
polo shirt	el polo
shorts	el short / pantalón corto
socks	los calcetines
T-shirt	la camiseta / el niki
trainers	las zapatillas (de deporte)
sweatshirt	la sudadera

jewellery *la joyería*

bracelet	la pulsera
brooch	el prendedor / broche
earrings	los pendientes
necklace	el collar
ring	el anillo
watch	el reloj
gold	el oro
silver	la plata
platinum	el platino
diamond	el diamante
emerald	la esmeralda
ruby	el rubí
sapphire	el zafiro
semi-precious stone	la piedra semipreciosa

Useful verbs

| to wear | llevar (puesto) |

Useful phrases

he / she always looks …	él / ella siempre parece …
casual	informal
fashionable	de moda
smart	elegante
unfashionable	pasado de moda
untidy	descuidado

10.4 Footwear

Core vocabulary

the shoe shop	*la zapatería*
footwear	el calzado
hosiery	la calcetería
socks	los calcetines
stockings	las medias
tights	los pantis
boots	las botas
clogs	los zuecos / chanclos
flip flops	las chancletas
moccasins	los mocasines
sandals	las sandalias
shoes	los zapatos
slip ons	los zapatos sin cordones
slippers	las zapatillas
tennis shoes	las zapatillas de tenis
trainers	las zapatillas (de deporte)
wellington / rubber boots	las botas de agua / goma
ballet shoes	las zapatillas de ballet
climbing boots	las botas de alpinismo / escalada
cycling shoes	las zapatillas de ciclismo
dancing shoes	los zapatos de baile
diving boots	las botas de buceo
flippers	las aletas
ski boots	las botas de esquí
snowboard boots	las botas de snow(board)
steel-tipped boots	las botas con punteras de acero
walking boots	las botas para andar

leather	el cuero
rubber	la goma
synthetics	la fibra sintética
high-heeled shoes	los zapatos de tacón alto
flat shoes	los zapatos planos
shoe polish	el betún
shoe cleaner	la crema para zapatos
shoe stretcher	el ensanchador para zapatos
chiropody	la podología / pedicura
massage	el masaje
reflexology	la reflexología / reflejoterapia
foot	el pie
toe	el dedo del pie
ankle	el tobillo
sole (of foot)	la planta
sole (of shoe)	la suela
toe nail	la uña del dedo del pie
arch of the foot	el puente del pie

Useful verbs

to try shoes on	probarse unos zapatos
to put on your shoes	ponerse los zapatos
to take off your shoes	quitarse los zapatos
to get blisters	ampollarse

Useful phrases

bare foot	descalzo
I have got sore feet.	Me duelen los pies.
I have got blisters.	Tengo ampollas en los pies.
Have you got a plaster?	¿Tiene(s) un esparadrapo / una tirita?
Please remove your shoes in the house.	Por favor, quítate / quítese los zapatos en la casa.
What shoe size are you?	¿Qué número (de zapato) calzas / gastas?
These shoes are comfortable / uncomfortable.	Estos zapatos (no) son cómodos.

11

travel

11.1 Travel

Core vocabulary

itinerary	el itinerario
journey	el viaje
map	el mapa
route	la ruta
travel	los viajes
overland	por tierra
by air	por avión
by sea	por mar
by rail	por ferrocarril
by train	en tren
by coach	en autocar
by car	en coche
by hire car	en un coche de alquiler
by boat	en barco
by ferry	en ferry
by bike	en bicicleta
on horseback	a caballo
on foot	a pie / andando
timetable	el horario
ticket	el billete
booking	la reserva
reservation	la reserva
on-line booking	la reserva por internet / on-line
arrival	la llegada
departure	la salida

Useful verbs

to travel	viajar
to go	ir
to sail	navegar
to fly	volar
to drive	viajar en coche
to tour	viajar / ir de gira
to arrive	llegar
to leave (transport)	salir
to leave (person)	irse / marcharse

Useful phrases

Can you help me please?	¿Me puede ayudar? / Ayúdeme por favor.
I'm lost.	Me he perdido.
How do I get to …?	¿Cómo puedo ir a …?
What is the best way to go to …?	¿Cuál es la mejor ruta para …?
Is it far?	¿Está lejos?
How far is it?	¿A qué distancia está?
How long does it take?	¿Cuánto tiempo se lleva para ir allí?

11.2 Travel by train

Core vocabulary

station	la estación
station master	el jefe de estación
booking office	el despacho de billetes
timetable	el horario
ticket	el billete
single ticket	el billete de ida
return ticket	el billete de ida y vuelta

types of ticket

tipos de billete

child	de niño
adult	de adulto / mayor
family	familiar
senior / pensioners	de jubilados / pensionistas
group	de grupo
arrivals	llegadas
departures	salidas
indicator board	el tablero de anuncios
information	la información
waiting room	la sala de espera
platform	el andén
subway	el paso subterráneo
stairs	la escalera
lift	el ascensor
line	la línea
train	el tren
express	el rápido

Intercity	el Íntercity
local / slow	el tren de cercanías
underground	el metro
coach	el vagón
non-smoking	de no fumadores
first class	de primera clase
buffet	el vagón restaurante
personnel	el personal
guard	el jefe de tren
ticket inspector	el revisor
train driver	el maquinista
passenger	el pasajero
traveller	el viajero
level crossing	el paso a nivel
railway track	la vía (férrea)
signals	los semáforos (de ferrocarril)
luggage	el equipaje
suitcase	la maleta
left luggage	la consigna

Useful verbs

to book a ticket	reservar un billete
to make a reservation	hacer una reserva

Useful phrases

Do I have to change?	¿Tengo que cambiar?
Is the train on time?	¿El tren, llega puntual?
How late is the train?	¿Qué retraso lleva el tren?
Will I miss the connection?	¿Perderé el enlace?
Is there a car park at the station?	¿Hay un aparcamiento en la estación?
Which platform does it leave from?	¿De qué andén sale?
Is this the train for ...?	¿Este es el tren para ...?
This is my place.	Este es mi asiento.
I have a reservation.	Tengo (una) reserva.
How often does it run?	¿Con cuánta frecuencia circula ...?
Which line do I need for ...?	¿Qué línea tengo que tomar para ...?

11.3 Travel by plane

Core vocabulary

airport	el aeropuerto
car park	el aparcamiento
departures	(las) salidas
check-in desk	el mostrador de facturación
luggage search	registro de equipaje
security check	control de seguridad
departure lounge	sala de embarque
executive lounge	sala para ejecutivos
information	información
announcements	anuncios / avisos
economy	clase económica / turista
business	clase preferente
first	primera clase
ticket	el billete
passport	el pasaporte
visa	el visado
green card	la carta verde
flight	el vuelo
gate	la puerta
delay	el retraso
plane	el avión
row	la fila
seat	el asiento
window seat	el asiento junto a la ventana
aisle seat	el asiento de pasillo
seat belt	el cinturón de seguridad
life jacket	el chaleco salvavidas
emergency exit	la salida de emergencia
toilet	el lavabo
Can I have ...?	¿Me da ...? ¿Puede darme ...?
earphones	los auriculares
a blanket	una manta
a pillow	una almohada
a glass of water	un vaso de agua
arrivals	llegadas
baggage reclaim	recogida de equipaje
customs	la aduana
duty	derechos de Aduana

pilot	el piloto
steward	el auxiliar de vuelo
stewardess	la azafata

Useful verbs

to leave / depart	salir
to take off	despegar
to fly	volar
to land	aterrizar
to arrive	llegar
to navigate	navegar
to put the seat back	echar el asiento hacia atrás
to put the seat upright	poner el asiento hacia delante
to stow the table	guardar la mesilla plegable
to experience turbulence	entrar en un área de turbulencias

Useful phrases

The plane is delayed.	El avión lleva un retraso.
Your flight leaves from gate ...	Su vuelo sale de la puerta número ...
Please will you return to your seats and fasten your seatbelts.	Por favor, vuelvan a sus asientos y pónganse los cinturones de seguridad.
We are flying at an altitude of ...	Volamos a una altura de ...
And a speed of ...	Y a una velocidad de ...
My luggage is missing.	Falta mi equipaje.

11.4 Travel by car

car	el coche
estate car	el coche familiar / la ranchera
four-wheel drive	con tracción en las cuatro ruedas
off-road car	coche todoterreno
sports car	el coche deportivo
convertible	el coche descapatable
automatic	automático

it has ...	tiene ...
2/4 doors	2/4 puertas
16 valves	16 válvulas

pedals	los pedales
accelerator	el acelerador
brake	el freno
clutch	el embrague

windscreen	el parabrisas
gears	las velocidades / las marchas
gear lever	la palanca de cambios
the steering wheel	el volante
the handbrake	el freno de mano
the indicators	los intermitentes
the lights	las luces
headlamps	los faros
side lights	las luces laterales
on full	las luces largas
on dip	las luces cortas

the speedometer	el velocímetro
the mileometer	el cuentakilómetros
the petrol gauge	el indicador del nivel de gasolina

the interior / *el interior*

seats	los asientos
safety belt	el cinturón de seguridad
leg room	el sitio para las piernas
glove compartment	la guantera
visor / sunshield	la visera
wing mirror	el retrovisor
rearview mirror	el espejo retrovisor
heating	la calefacción
air conditioning	el aire acondicionado
wheel	la rueda / llanta
tyre	el neumático
valve	la válvula
tyre pressure	la presión de los neumáticos
jack	el gato
spare wheel	la rueda de repuesto

the exterior / *el exterior*

boot	el maletero
bumper	el parachoques

number plate	la matrícula
foglights	los faros antiniebla
rear lights	las luces traseras
exhaust	el escape
battery	la batería
radiator	el radiador
ignition	el encendido
spark plug	la bujía
oil pressure	la presión del aceite
fan belt	la correa del ventilador
windscreen wiper	el limpiaparabrisas
windscreen washer	el lavaparabrisas
warning light	la señal luminosa
gears	las marchas / velocidades

Useful verbs

to drive	conducir / llevar el coche
to put your lights on	poner las luces
to turn your lights off	apagar las luces
to put your indicator on	poner el intermitente
to give way	ceder el paso
to overtake	adelantar

11.5 The road

Core vocabulary

a road	una carretera
a country road	un camino de campo / rural
a main road	una carretera principal
a one-way road	una carretera de sentido único / dirección única
a dual carriageway	una autovía / carretera de doble calzada
motorway	una autopista
motorway lane	un carril de la autopista
inside lane	el carril de la derecha
outside lane	el carril de la izquierda
central reservation	la mediana
access road	la vía de acceso

- Most motorways in Spain are toll roads. It is a good idea to have enough change ready when you get to a **peaje,** but in most cases you can pay with a credit card.
- Note that an **autovía** is a near motorway-standard dual carriageway, with no tolls.

the road surface is ...	la calzada / el firme es ...
good / bad	buena / mala
smooth / uneven	igual / desigual
bumpy	lleno de baches
intersection	el enlace cruce
crossroad	la encrucijada
T-junction	el cruce en T
roundabout	el cruce giratorio / la glorieta
bridge	el puente
toll bridge	el puente de peaje
level crossing	el paso a nivel
traffic lights	los semáforos

Note that Spanish traffic lights go straight from red to green, with no red + amber phase.

road works	las obras
emergency traffic lights	los semáforos de emergencia
the diversion	la desviación / el desvío
road signs	las señales de tráfico
crawler lane	el carril para vehículos lentos
hard shoulder	el arcén
speed limit	el límite de velocidad
speed camera	la cámara electrónica de velocidad
traffic police	la policía de tráfico
driving licence	el permiso de conducir
insurance	el seguro
fine	la multa
services	el área (f) de servicio
garage (for repairs / service)	el taller
petrol station	la estación de servicio / la gasolinera
petrol	la gasolina
diesel	el diesel
air	el aire
water	el agua
oil	el aceite
oil change	el cambio de aceite

emergency services	los servicios de emergencia / urgencia
breakdown	la avería

Useful verbs

to speed	conducir por encima del límite de velocidad permitido
to accelerate	acelerar
to slow down	reducir la velocidad
to brake	frenar
to break down	averiarse

Useful phrases

I have broken down.	Mi coche está averiado.
The car is overheating.	Se sobrecalienta el coche.
The engine has stopped.	El motor ha dejado de funcionar / andar.
I have a puncture.	Tengo un pinchazo.

12

tourism

12.1 Where to go

Core vocabulary

tourism industry	la industria turística, el turismo
travel agency	la agencia de viajes
a brochure	un folleto
the tourist	el / la turista
excursion	una excursión
tour	una gira
coach trip	una excursión en autocar
guided visit	una visita con guía
cruise	un crucero
holiday resort	el lugar de veraneo
seaside	la playa / orilla del mar
sea, sand and sun	el mar, la arena y el sol
mountains and lakes	montañas y lagos
countryside	el campo / paisaje
adventure holiday	la vacaciones de aventura
winter sports	los deportes de invierno
outdoor pursuits	las actividades al aire libre
peak season holidays	vacaciones durante períodos de máxima demanda
national holiday	la fiesta nacional
to go on holiday	ir de vacaciones
to go on summer holiday	veranear

- If you travel around Spain, especially by road, you will almost certainly at some stage come across a town or village in *fiesta*: every place has its patron saint, on whose feast-day there will be celebrations – usually consisting of music, dancing food and drink, as well as a (usually religious) procession. Many areas have their own specialities.
- Cataluña has many *fiestas* celebrating the national dance, the *sardana*, which is also danced on Sunday mornings in front of Barcelona cathedral.
- Valencia has an annual festival based on the ancient water laws, and another in March called *las Fallas* at which huge effigies are burned.
- The region south of Valencia celebrates the victories of Christians against Moors – *Moros y Cristianos* – with mock battles and processions.
- Andalucía has many colourful *fiestas* such as *Las Cruces de mayo* in Granada, and the *Fiesta de abril* in Sevilla.

- Madrid celebrates the feast of *San Isidro* with a festival of bullfighting, while Pamplona has the annual bull-running through the streets to celebrate *San Fermín* in July.

All over Spain, national festivals are celebrated such as the following:
- *Semana Santa* – a week of often sombre religious processions leading up to Easter
- *el día de la Hispanidad* celebrated on the day of *La Virgen del Pilar* on October 12 – Spain's national day
- *el día de los Reyes* celebrating the Epiphany and the three kings (Magi) on January 6; there are processions in which the kings throw sweets to the children, and that night children leave their shoes on the balcony, to be filled with presents by the *Reyes Magos*.

12.2 What to take

Core vocabulary

luggage	el equipaje
suitcase	la maleta
travel bag	el bolso de viaje
overnight bag	el bolso de viaje
rucksack	la mochila
hand luggage	el equipaje de mano
passport	el pasaporte
visa	el visado
tickets	los billetes
insurance	el seguro
driving licence	el permiso de conducir
credit card	la tarjeta de crédito
currency	la moneda
travellers cheques	los cheques de viaje / viajero
emergency phone number	número de teléfono de urgencia / emergencia
laptop	el ordenador portátil
mobile phone	el (teléfono) móvil
sponge bag	la esponjera
toilet bag	el neceser
soap	el jabón
toothbrush	el cepillo de dientes
toothpaste	la pasta de dientes

razor	la maquinilla de afeitar
electric razor	la máquina de afeitar
nail scissors	las tijeras para las uñas
tweezers	las pinzas
shampoo	el champú
conditioner	el suavizante / acondicionador
hairbrush	el cepillo para el pelo / cabello
comb	el peine
face cream	la crema para la cara
hand cream	la crema para las manos
cleanser	la crema limpiadora
moisturiser	la crema hidratante
sun cream	el bronceador
waterproof sun cream	el bronceador resistente al agua
aftersun cream	la crema para después de broncearse???
wardrobe	el armario
coat hanger	la percha
iron	la plancha

Useful verbs

to pack	hacer la(s) maleta(s)
to unpack	deshacer la(s) maleta(s)
to fold	plegar
to hang up	colgar
to wash	lavar
to dry clean	lavar en seco
to mend	remendar / zurcir
to press / iron	planchar

Useful phrases

I have lost my luggage.	He perdido mi equipaje.
I can't find ...	No encuentro ...
Have you got a ...?	¿Tiene(s) (usted) un(a) ...?
Where can I get a ...?	¿Dónde puedo obtener / comprar / encontrar un(a) ...?
Where is the nearest ...?	¿Dónde está el / la .... más cerca de aquí?

12.3 Where to stay

Core vocabulary

accommodation	***el alojamiento***
two-star hotel	un hotel de dos estrellas
three-star hotel	un hotel de tres estrellas
luxury hotel	un hotel de lujo
inn	la taberna / posada / el mesón
bed and breakfast	pensión con desayuno*
holiday house / home	la casa para ocupar durante las vacaciones
youth hostel	el albergue juvenil
campsite	el camping
caravan site	el camping para caravanas

*In most Spanish boarding houses, you just pay for the bed; breakfast is usually not available – you have to go to a nearby bar or café for your breakfast.

entrance	la entrada
reception	la recepción
night porter	el guarda nocturno
manager	el director / gerente
staff	el personal
porter	el portero
bill	la cuenta
single room	una habitación individual / sencilla
room with a double bed	una habitación doble (con cama) de matrimonio
twin-bedded room	una habitación doble (con dos camas)
family room	una habitación familiar
with shower	con ducha
with bathroom	con baño
with toilet	con wáter / retrete
with phone	con teléfono
with television	con televisor
with internet connection	con conexión de Internet
with a balcony	con balcón
with a sea view	con vista al mar
with air conditioning	con aire acondicionado
reception	la recepción
stairs	la escalera

lift	el ascensor
restaurant	el restaurante
fitness room	el gimnasio
pool	la piscina
hot tub	el jacuzzi

Useful phrases

Have you got ...?	¿Tiene(n) ...?
anything bigger / smaller	algo más grande / pequeño
anything cheaper / better	algo más barato / mejor
anything quieter	algo más tranquilo
a non-smoking room	una habitación para no fumadores
It is too noisy.	Es demasiado ruidoso.
The shower doesn't work.	No funciona la ducha.
There is no hot water.	No hay agua caliente.
There is no plug in the sink.	No hay tapón en el lavabo.

12.4 Camping and caravanning

Core vocabulary

camp site	el camping
caravan	la caravana
camper van	la autocaravana
trailer	el remolque
tent	la tienda (de campaña)
frame tent	la tienda familiar
site	el sitio
a flat site	un sitio plano
a shady site	un sitio sombreado

tent	*la tienda (de campaña)*
tent peg	la estaca (de tienda)
tent pole	el palo
guy rope	la cuerda (de la tienda)
groundsheet	el aislante / suelo de tienda
sleeping bag	el saco de dormir
torch	la linterna
blanket	la manta

gas cooker	la cocina de gas portátil / el cámping gas
gas bottle	el butano / la bomba de gas

facilities | ***las instalaciones***
electricity	la electricidad / la luz
power socket	la toma de corriente / el enchufe
water	el agua (f)
running water	el agua corriente
drinking water	el agua potable
water tap	el grifo de agua
washrooms	los servicios / los aseos
toilet	el aseo / el servicio
shower	la ducha
wash basin	el lavabo
hair dryers	los secadores de pelo
cooking area	la cocina
gas rings	el fuego de gas
washing-up sinks	las pilas para lavar platos
washing machines	las lavadoras
clothes driers	las secadoras
drying area	la zona para tender ropa
restaurant	el restaurante
bar	el bar
shop	la tienda
swimming pool	la piscina
paddling pool	la piscina para niños
children's play area	la zona de recreo para niños
swings	los columpios
slide	el tobogán
roundabout	el carrusel

Useful verbs

to tow	remolcar
to park	aparcar
to put up	montar
to take down	desmontar
to hook up (connect)	enchufar / conectar
to get wet	mojarse
to wash / do the washing	lavar la ropa
to dry	secar

Useful phrases

Can you help me?	¿Me puede ayudar?
I don't understand how the … works.	No entiendo cómo funciona el / la …
Where is the …?	¿Dónde está el / la …?
Is there electricity / water / shade…?	¿Hay electricidad / agua / sombra?
Do you have …?	¿Tiene(s) (usted) …?
When is the shop open?	¿A qué hora se abre la tienda?
Where can I get …?	¿Dónde puedo conseguir / obtener …?

12.5 What are you going to do?

we want to go …

queremos ir a …

swimming	la natación
diving	el salto de trampolín
water skiing	el esquí acuático
surfing	el surf
walking	el excursionismo
hiking	el excursionismo (a pie)
climbing	el montañismo / alpinismo
gliding	el planeo / vuelo sin motor
paragliding	el parapente
hanggliding	el vuelo con ala delta
do sport	hacer el deporte
play tennis	jugar al tenis
play volleyball	jugar al voleibol
go bike riding	hacer ciclismo

we want to see …

queremos ver …

the sights	los sitios de interés
monuments	los monumentos
castles	los castillos
archeological sites	los sitios arqueológicos
ancient monuments	los monumentos antiguos
historic buildings	los edificios históricos
the scenery	el paisaje
animals	los animales

we want …

queremos …

to have a good time	pasarlo bien / divertirnos*

to have a rest	descansar(nos)*
to relax	relajar(nos)*
sun, sea and sand	sol, mar y arena
to do nothing	no hacer nada
to be waited on	ser atendidos
to find some sun	encontrar el sol

*These expressions are reflexive, and we have put the pronoun into the **nos** form, which is what you will need after queremos ...

in winter I like to go ... / **en el invierno me gusta ir a hacer ...**

skiing	el esquí
snowboarding	el snowboard
sledging	el trineo
ice skating	el patinaje sobre hielo
ice climbing	escalar en hielo

Useful phrases

What is there to see / do?	¿Qué hay para ver / hacer?
Is it suitable for ...?	¿Es apto para ...?
older people	las personas mayores / ancianos
younger people	(los) jóvenes
children	(los) niños

12.6 On the beach

Core vocabulary

sea	el mar
coast	la costa
beach	la playa
bay	la bahía
shore	la orilla
sand	la arena
rocks	las rocas
rock pools	las charcas entre rocas
seashells	las conchas
tide	la marea
waves	las olas

private / public beach	la playa privada / pública
beach bar	la chiringuito
wind break	el cotavientos
shelter	el refugio
parasol	la sombrilla / el parasol
lounger	la tumbona
deck chair	la tumbona
air mattress	el colchón inflable
shower	la ducha
towel	la toalla
swimming costume	el traje de baño
trunks	el bañador
bikini	el bikini
suntan lotion	el bronceador
total screen / sunblock	el filtro solar
sun glasses	las gafas de sol
rubber ring	el flotador
arm bands	los brazaletes
sandcastle	el castillo de arena
bucket	el cubito
spade	la pala
kite	la cometa
snorkel	el esnórquel
flippers	la aleta
wet suit	el traje isotérmico
dry suit	el traje seco
inflatable	inflable / hinchable
hand / foot pump	la bomba de mano / pie
surf board	la tabla / plancha de surf
wind surfer	el windsurfista
jetski	la moto acuática
waterski	el esquí acuático
fish (live)	el pez
fish (caught/dead)	el pescado
shells	las conchas
octopus	el pulpo
squid	el calamar
mussels	el mejillón
scallops	las veneras
shrimps	los camarones
jellyfish	la medusa

Useful verbs

to snorkel	hacer el esnórquel
to sunbathe	tomar el sol
to relax	relajar(se) (*reflexive*)
to play	jugar
to dig	cavar
to dive	tirarse (al agua)
to sting	picar
to waterski	hacer el esquí acuático

Useful phrases

The tide is in / out.	La marea está alta / baja.
It is safe for bathing / swimming.	Es seguro para bañarse / nadar.
I have been stung by a jellyfish.	Me ha picado una medusa.
He / She is out of her depth.	Él / ella no hace fondo / pie.
He / She can't swim.	Él / ella no sabe nadar.
He / She needs help.	Necesita ayuda.
Help!	¡Socorro!

12.7 At sea

Core vocabulary

canoe	la piragua
jetski	la moto acuática
motor boat	la lancha a motor
outboard (motor)	(el motor) fuera bordo
RIB (rigid inflatable boat)	el zodiac
rubber dinghy	la lancha neumática
rowing boat	la barca de remos
sailing dinghy	el bote de vela
surf board	la plancha de surf
waterski	el esquí acuático
windsurfer	el windsurfista
yacht	el velero
emergency services	los servicios de urgencia / emergencia
lifeboat (from shore)	la lancha de socorro
lifeboat (from ship)	el bote salvavidas

lifejacket	el chaleco salvavidas
lifeguard	el salvavidas
flare	la bengala
weather forecast	el pronóstico del tiempo
the sea is ...	el mar está ...
calm	en calma / tranquilo
rough	agitado
wind force	la fuerza del viento
gale force wind	el viento huracanado
rain	la lluvia
poor / good visibility	poca / buena visibilidad
fog	la niebla
equipment	el equipo
compass	la brújula
sails	las velas
hull	el casco
cabin	el camarote
berth	la litera
wheel	el timón
harbour	el puerto
port	el puerto
lighthouse	el faro
port	(a) babor
starboard	(a) estribor
mooring	el amarradero
buoy	la boya
chain	la cadena
anchor	el ancla (f)

Useful verbs

to sail	navegar
to navigate	navegar
to steer	gobernar
to tie up / moor	amarrar
to anchor	anclar
to rescue	rescatar
to be rescued	ser rescatado/a ...

12.8 The great outdoors

Core vocabulary

rucksack	la mochila
sleeping bag	el saco de dormir
ground mat / mattress	el colchón inflable
torch	la linterna
penknife	la navaja
compass	la brújula
map	el mapa
water bottle	la cantimplora
camping stove	la cocina de gas portátil / el cámping gas
matches	los fósforos / las cerillas
lighter	el encendedor / la mechera
gas container	el butano / la bomba de gas
billycan (for cooking on stove)	el cazo
bowl	el plato
knife / fork / spoon	el cuchillo / el tenedor / la cuchara
plate	el plato
mug	el tazón
emergency rations	las raciones de reserva
dried food	los comestibles secos
dried fruit	las frutas pasas
nuts	las nueces
chocolate	el chocolate
transceiver (for snow rescue)	el transceptor / el transmisor–receptor
mobile phone	el teléfono móvil
batteries	las pilas
charger	el cargador
plug	el enchufe
waterproofs	la ropa impermeable
spare clothing	la ropa de reserva
rope	la cuerda
climbing harness	el arnés de montañismo
climbing gear	el equipo de montañismo
crampons	los garfios
boots	las botas

ice axe	la piqueta (de alpinista)
sore feet	los pies doloridos / lastimados
spare socks	calcetines de reserva
blisters	las ampollas
plasters	los esparadrapos / las tiritas
antiseptic cream	la crema antiséptica
insect repellent	el repelente contra insectos
antihistamine cream (for insect bites)	la crema antihistamínica

Useful phrases

Have you got ...?	¿Tiene(s) ...?
Have you got something for ...?	¿Tiene(s) algo para ...?
I have been stung by a wasp / bee	Me ha picado una avispa / una abeja.
I have been bitten by ...	Me ha mordido ...
a mosquito	un mosquito
a snake	una serpiente
a dog	un perro

13

the body and health

13.1 The face

Core vocabulary

head	la cabeza
face	la cara
hair	el pelo / cabello
forehead	la frente
ears	las orejas
eyes	los ojos
eyebrows	los párpados
eyelashes	las cejas
nose	la nariz
nostrils	las narices
cheeks	las mejillas
chin	la barbilla
mouth	la boca
lips	los labios
tongue	la lengua
teeth	los dientes
neck	el cuello

toiletries — *artículos de tocador*

shampoo	el champú
conditioner	el acondiconador / suavizante
face cream	la crema facial
moisturiser	la crema hidratante
face pack	la mascarilla facial
lip salve	el protector labial
shaving cream	la crema de afeitar
shaving brush	la brocha de afeitar
razor	la navaja
electric razor	la máquina de afeitar
after-shave lotion	la loción para después del afeitado
make-up	el maquillaje
mascara	el rímel
lipstick	la barra de labios
eye shadow	la sombra de ojos
powder	los polvos

Useful phrases

He has a beard.	Tiene / Lleva una barba.
moustache	(el) bigote
He / she wears glasses	Él / Ella lleva gafas.
contact lenses	las lentes de contacto
I am short-sighted.	Soy miope.
long-sighted	présbita
I have a headache.	Me duele la cabeza. / Tengo dolor de cabeza.
toothache	el dolor de dientes
earache	el dolor de oído(s)
a nose bleed	una hemorragía nasal
My eyes are sore	Me duelen los ojos.
to have a facial	hacer un tratamiento facial
to have your hair done	arreglarse el pelo
to have a nose job	operarse la nariz
to have plastic surgery	hacerse la cirugía plástica / cosmética
to have wrinkles	tener arrugas
to have a nice smile	tener una sonrisa bonita

Useful verbs

to hear	oír
to see	ver
to smell	oler
to taste	gustar
to wink	guiñar
to sleep	dormir
to smile	sonreír
to laugh	reír
to talk	hablar
to shout	gritar
to cry	llorar
to snore	roncar
to hiccup	hipar
to cough	toser

13.2 The body

shoulders	el hombro
back	la espalda

arms	el brazo
elbow	el codo
wrist	la muñeca
hands	la mano
finger	el dedo
thumb	el pulgar
fingernail	la uña
body	el cuerpo
chest	el pecho
breasts	los pechos
nipples	los pezones
waist	la cintura / el talle
hips	las caderas
abdomen	el abdomen
bottom	el trasero
the sexual organs	los órganos sexuales
the penis	el pene
the balls	los cojones
the vagina	la vagina
legs	las piernas
thighs	los muslos
knees	las rodillas
calves	las pantorrillas
ankle	el tobillo
foot	el pie
toes	los dedos del pie
arch	el puente
heel	el tacón
the back	el dorso
the front	la parte delantera
the side	el lado

internal organs — *los órganos internos*

brain	el cerebro
stomach	el estómago
throat	la garganta
lungs	los pulmones
kidneys	los riñones
heart	el corazón
blood	la sangre
the veins	las venas
the arteries	las arterias
intestines	los intestinos

skeleton	el esqueleto
bones	los huesos
joints	las coyunturas
nervous system	el sistema nervioso
nerves	los nervios
circulation	la circulación
breathing	la respiración
digestion	la digestión

Useful verbs

to feel	sentir(se) (*reflexive*)
to touch	tocar
to stroke	acariciar
to massage	dar un masaje
to hold	agarrar
to embrace	abrazar(se)
to kiss	besar
to make love	hacer el amor
to kick	dar patadas (a)
to walk	andar / ir andando
to run	correr
to jump	saltar

13.3 I need to see a doctor

Core vocabulary

doctor	el médico
appointment	la cita
surgery	la consulta
immunization	la inmunización
innoculation	la inoculación
a health certificate	un certificado de salud
an examination	un reconocimiento
ailments	***las enfermedades***
a cold	un resfriado
flu (influenza)	la gripe
measles	el sarampión
mumps	las paperas
German measles	la rubeola
tonsillitis	la amigdalitis
a cough	una tos
sore throat	un dolor de garganta

indigestion	la indigestión
hypertension	la hipertensión
constipation	la estreñimiento
diarrhoea	la diarrea
polio	la polio(mielitis)
hepatitis	la hepatitis
rabies	la rabia
typhoid	la tifoidea
cholera	la cólera
yellow fever	la fiebre amarilla
malaria	la malaria
cancer	el cáncer
multiple sclerosis	la esclerosis múltiple
medicine	la medicina
pills	las pastillas
pain relief	el alivio contra el dolor
vitamin supplements	los suplementos vitamínicos
cure	la cura
homeopathic remedy	el remedio homeopático
exercise	el ejercicio
physiotherapy	la fisioterapia
rest	el descanso
sleep	el sueño
go to bed	ve / vaya a la cama / acuéstate / acuéstese (*reflexive*)
sleep	duerme / duerma
take more exercise	toma / tome / haz / haga más ejercicio
eat less	come / coma menos
avoid	evita / evite ...

Useful phrases

I have a pain ...	Me duele / Tengo (un) dolor (de) ...
It hurts / They hurt.	Me duele / Me duelen.
I don't feel well.	No me siento bien.
I can't sleep / eat / walk ...	No puedo dormir / comer / andar.
I want to go to the toilet.	Quiero ir al lavabo / a los aseos / servicios.

I feel sick.	Me siento enfermo / tengo náuseas.
I feel dizzy.	Me siento mareado.
I have got spots.	Tengo granos en la piel.
I have been bitten / stung.	Se me ha picado.
I have stomach ache.	Tengo dolor de estómago.
heart burn	la acidez
indigestion	la indigestión
high / low blood pressure	la tensión (de sangre) alta/baja
My foot / hand / leg hurts	Me duele el pie / la mano / la pierna.
I am allergic to ...	Soy alérgico a ...
penicillin	la penicilina
nuts	las nueces
animals	los animales
I have hay fever.	Tengo fiebre del heno.
asthma	el asma
He needs an inhaler.	Él necesita un inhalador.
She is handicapped.	Ella es minusválida.
paraplegic	parapléjico
an injection / a jab for	una inyección para ...
I have broken my leg / ankle / wrist ...	me he roto la pierna / el tobillo / la muñeca
plaster	la escayola
crutches	las muletas
walking stick	el bastón
wheel chair	la silla de ruedas

13.4 At the hospital

Core vocabulary

hospital	el hospital
department	el departamento
emergency	la emergencia / urgencia
doctor	el médico
nurse	la enfermera / el enfermero
ward	la sala
bed	la cama
anaesthetic	el anestésico
surgery (medical procedure)	la cirugía

surgery (place)	la clínica / consulta
operation	la operación / intervención quirúrgica
operating theatre	el quirófano / la sala de operaciones
a blood transfusion	una transfusión de sangre
a blood donor	un donador de sangre
my blood type	mi grupo sanguíneo
an x-ray	un rayo X
radiation	la radiación

13.5 Contraception

family planning	la planificación familiar
contraception	la anticoncepción
condom	el preservativo
the coil	el espiral
the pill	la píldora
the morning-after pill	la píldora del día después
vasectomy	la vasectomía

14

the world

14.1 Countries

Core vocabulary

world	el mundo
earth	la tierra
globe	el globo
atlas	el atlas
country	el país

the continents and major regions	*los continentes*
Africa	África
North America	América del Norte
South America	América del Sur
Asia	Asia
Australia	Australia
Europe	Europa
Antarctica	Antárctico
America	América
Arctic	el Ártico
Middle East	el Oriente Medio
Far East	el Lejano Oriente / Extremo Oriente
Pacific rim	(los países de) la Costa del Pacífico
Indo-China	Indochina
India	India
China	China
Japan	el Japón
Indonesia	Indonesia
Australasia	Australasia
New Zealand	Nueva Zelandia / Zelanda
the Pacific Islands	las Islas del Pacífico

14.2 The countries of Europe

Core vocabulary

Scandinavia	*Escandinavia*
Denmark	Dinamarca
Finland	Finlandia

Norway	Noruega
Sweden	Suecia
Iceland	Islandia

the Low Countries — ***los Países Bajos***
Belgium	Bélgica
Holland	Holanda
Luxembourg	Luxemburgo

the Iberian Peninsula — ***la Península Ibérica***
Spain	España
Portugal	Portugal

the United Kingdom — ***el Reino Unido***
England	Inglaterra
Scotland	Escocia
Northern Ireland	Irlanda del Norte
Wales	el País de Gales

Europe — ***Europa***
Greece	Grecia
Turkey	Turquía
Germany	Alemania
Poland	Polonia
France	Francia
Ireland	Irlanda
Austria	Austria
Italy	Italia
the Czech Republic	la República Checa
Hungary	Hungría
Slovakia	Eslovaquia
Switzerland	Suiza

the European Union — ***la Unión Europea***
the European Parliament	el Parlamento Europeo
the Common Market	el Mercado Común
Member of the European Parliament	Diputado del Parlamento Europeo / eurodiputado
the Common Agricultural Policy	la Política Agrícola Común
the euro	el euro
the European institutions	las instituciones europeas
the European bank	el Banco Europeo

14.3 The high seas

Core vocabulary

the points of the compass	*las cuartas de la brújula*
north	norte (+ noreste, noroeste)
south	sur (+ sureste, suroeste)
east	este
west	oeste

the oceans	*los océanos*
Atlantic	el Atlántico
Indian	el Océano Índico
Pacific	el Pacífico
Mediterranean	el Mediterráneo
North Sea	el Mar del Norte
Baltic	el mar Báltico
Red Sea	el Mar Rojo
English Channel	el Canal de la Mancha

navigation	la navegación
longitude	la longitud
latitude	la latitud
equator	el ecuador
northern hemisphere	el hemisferio norte
southern hemisphere	el hemisferio sur
tropics	el trópico
bay	la bahía
island	la isla
peninsula	la península
canal	el canal
the Suez canal	el Canal de Suez
the Panama canal	el Canal de Panamá
straits	el estrecho
currents	las corrientes
tides	las mareas

ferry	el ferry / el transbordador
liner	el transatlántico
cruise ship	el crucero
tanker	el petrolero
container ship	el portacontenedores

hazard	el peligro
iceberg	el iceberg
shipping	los barcos / la navegación

shipping forecast	el pronóstico marítimo
storm	la tormenta / la tempestad
gale	el vendaval
gale force (ten)	el vientos huracanados (de fuerza diez)
rough sea	el mar agitado / la fuerte marejada
calm sea	el mar tranquilo

Useful verbs

to board	ir a bordo
to embark	embarcar
to disembark	desembarcar

14.4 The weather forecast

Core vocabulary

weather forecast	el pronóstico del tiempo
rain	la lluvia
snow	la nieve
wind	el viento
fog	la niebla
sun	el sol
hail	la llovizna
sleet	la aguanieve
thunder	el trueno
lightning	el relámpago
It is ... raining	llueve / está lloviendo
snowing	nieva / está nevando
sunny	(está) soleado / (hace sol)
warm	caliente / caluroso
cold	frío
cloudy	nuboso
overcast	cubierto
rainy	lluvioso
wet / damp / humid	húmedo
mild	templado
dry	seco
It is cold	hace frío
hot	calor
good weather	buen tiempo
bad weather	mal tiempo

yesterday	ayer
today	hoy
tomorrow	mañana
over the next few days	en los próximos días
the weather is getting worse	el tiempo está empeorando
improving	mejorando
you can expect	se puede anticipar
light / strong winds	vientos débiles / flojos / fuertes
rain / snow	lluvia / nieve
clouds	nubes
gusts of wind	rachas de viento
gales	vendavales
storms	tormentas / tempestades
heavy showers	los chubascos
floods	inundaciones
sunny intervals	intervalos soleados
bright periods	intervalos claros
prolonged spells of rain	períodos prolongados de lluvia
morning mist	bruma matinal
fog patches	bancos de niebla
frost	escarcha / helada
dangerous driving conditions	condiciones peligrosas para conducir
risk of flooding	el riesgo de inundaciones
the temperature will be ...	la temperatura será ...
degrees	grados
celsius / centigrade	celsius / centígrado
fahrenheit	fahrenheit
the temperature is rising / falling	la temperatura sube / baja
maximum	máximo
minimum	mínimo

15

government and society

15.1 Politics and government

Core vocabulary

government	el gobierno
democracy	la democracia
state of law	el estado de derechos
dictatorship	la dictadura
monarchy	la monarquía
UK's parliamentary monarchy	la monarquía parlamentaria del Reino Unido
Spain's parliamentary democracy	la democracia parlamentaria de España

Spain's new democratic state is modelled on the UK system in being a constitutional parliamentary monarchy. King Juan Carlos is well-loved, having successfully smoothed the path of Spain's return to democracy in the last quarter of the twentieth century.

Spain has two main political parties:
- **Partido Popular** – which is currently in government. It stands for conservative values, a strong state, security and European commitment;
- **Partido Socialista Obrero Español** – this is the Socialist party, standing for social justice and equality, and very committed to Europe. During its time in power (1982–1996), this party introduced many social reforms.

King	(su majestad) el Rey
Queen	(su majestad) la Reina
King and Queen	los Reyes
Prince	el Príncipe
Princess	la Princesa
Head of State	el Jefe de Estado
President	el presidente (del Gobierno)
Prime Minister	el Primer Ministro
Head of Government	el Jefe del Gobierno

- The Spanish Prime Minister is also known as el presidente, being president of the government.
- The King, of course, is the **Jefe de Estado**, aided in official functions by the Queen and their family.
- The Spanish parliament – **las Cortes** – has two chambers: the **Congreso de los Diputados** is the lower house, members of which (**diputados**) are elected by proportional representation

for a four year term. The house elects its **presidente,** who is then invited by the King to form the government. The upper house is the **Senado,** whose members are called **senadores.**

cabinet	el Consejo de Ministros / el gabinete
Minister of the Interior	el Ministro del Interior
Defence Minister	el Ministro de Defensa
Chancellor of the Exchequer	el Ministro de Economía y Hacienda
Justice Minister	el Ministro de Justicia
parliament	el parlamento, las Cortes
chamber	la cámara
Lower House (Spanish Parliament)	el Congreso de los Diputados
Upper House (Spanish Parliament)	el Senado
member of elected parliament	el diputado
member of the higher chamber	el senador / miembro de la Cámara Alta
ministry	el ministerio
Foreign Office	el Ministerio de Asuntos Exteriores
Home Office	el Ministerio del Interior
Ministry of Education	el Ministerio de Educación
Ministry of Defence	el Ministerio de Defensa
constituency (area)	la circunscripción electoral / el distrito electoral
election	las elecciones (generales)
vote	el voto / la votación
the armed forces	las Fuerzas Armadas
the army	el Ejército
soldier / tank / to march	el soldado / un carro de combate / marchar
the navy	la Marina / Armada
sailor / warship / to sail	el marinero / el buque de guerra / navegar
the airforce	el Ejército del Aire
airman / pilot / jet fighter / to fly	el aviador / el piloto / el reactor / volar

Useful verbs

to appoint one's government	nombrar su gobierno
to appoint one's cabinet	nombrar su gabinete

to defend	defender
to fight	luchar (contra)
to guard	guarda
to protect	proteger
to spy	espiar
to speak	hablar
to make a speech	pronunciar un discurso
to canvass	solicitar el voto de …
to debate	debatir / discutir
to vote	votar
to pay taxes	pagar impuestos

15.2 Local government and services

Spain is divided into 13 regions (**Autonomías**), each with its own parliament and a certain degree of autonomy. Beneath this there is a structure of local government, with municipal authorities on the lowest level.

Core vocabulary

mayor	el alcalde
town / city councillor	el concejal
town hall	el ayuntamiento
local council	el concejo municipal
roads	las carreteras
transport	el transporte
tourist office	la oficina de turismo
council offices	las oficinas municipales
telephone	el teléfono
taxes	los impuestos
council tax	el impuesto municipal
rates	la contribución municipal
bureaucracy	la burocracia
the small print	la letra pequeña
red tape	el papeleo
civil servant	el funcionario
paperwork	el papeleo
permit	un permiso
certificate of residence	un permiso de residencia
receipt	un recibo
driving licence	un permiso de conducir

insurance	el seguro
medical insurance	el seguro médico
medical check	la revisión médica
solicitor	el procurador
lawyer	el abogado
criminal offence	el delito criminal
court	el tribunal / juzgado
sentence	la sentencia / condena
fine	la multa
imprisonment	el encarcelamiento
police	la policía
emergency services	los servicios de emergencia / urgencia
ambulance	la ambulancia
fire brigade	el Cuerpo de Bomberos
telephone	el teléfono
electricity	la electricidad / la luz (*common usage*)
gas	el gas
water	el agua
sewage	el sistema de depuración de aguas residuales

Useful phrases

I don't understand.	No entiendo.
I didn't know	No lo sabía.
I have already supplied you with this document.	Ya le he proporcionado ese documento.
I need help …	Necesito ayuda / que me ayuden …
Is there anyone who can help me?	¿Hay alguien que pueda ayudarme?
When are the offices open?	¿A qué hora se abren las oficinas?
Where do I need to go to get …?	¿Adónde tengo que ir para obtener …?
What do I need?	¿Qué necesito?
Where can I get it?	¿Dónde puedo obtenerlo/la?
a (rubber) stamp	la estampilla de goma
It has / hasn't been stamped.	No ha sido aprobado (oficialmente).

15.3 Money

Core vocabulary

currency	la moneda
dollars	los dólares
sterling	la libra esterlina
euros	los euros
cash	el (dinero) efectivo
bank	el banco
bank account	la cuenta bancaria
current account	la cuenta corriente
deposit	el depósito
account	la cuenta
account number	el número de la cuenta
bank sort code	el número de agencia
cheque book	el talonario
credit card	la tarjeta de crédito
cheque card	la tarjeta de identificación bancaria
signature	la firma
number / code	el número / código
loan	el préstamo / crédito
overdraft	el saldo deudor
bank transfer	la transferencia bancaria
in credit	con un saldo positivo
in the red	con un saldo negativo / en números rojos
bankruptcy	la quiebra
mortgage	la hipoteca
household insurance	el seguro doméstico
stocks and shares	las acciones
stock market	la bolsa
prices	los precios
dividend	el dividendo, los beneficios
profits	las ganancias
loss	la pérdida
inflation	la inflación
accounts	las cuentas
accountant	el contable
annual accounts	las cuentas anuales
income tax	el impuesto

Useful verbs

to apply	solicitar (ask for), presentarse
to be accepted	ser aceptado
to be refused	ser negado / rechazado
to win	ganar
to lose	perder
to make a gain	hacer ganancias / beneficios
to make a loss	hacer pérdidas
to buy / sell shares	comprar / vender ganancias
to save	ahorrar

The Spanish are great gamblers – they invest a considerable amount of money in their **Lotería Nacional**. Tickets – or rather tenths of tickets (**décimos**) are sold in special shops and kiosks. The jackpot prize **el Gordo** is one of the biggest prizes in the world. Winning numbers for the Christmas lottery are sung out by choirboys and the ceremony is broadcast on television.

15.4 National holidays

Core vocabulary

saint's day	el Santo
bank holidays	las fiestas nacionales
national holidays	las fiestas nacionales
local holidays	las fiestas locales
holidays	las fiestas nacionales
Christmas	(la) Navidad
New Year	el Año Nuevo
Easter	la Pascua (de Resurreción)
Easter Week / Holy Week	Semana Santa
Halloween	la víspera de Todos los Santos
January 6 - the Epiphany	el día de Reyes
Shrove Tuesday	Carnaval
Ash Wednesday	Miércoles de Ceniza
Good Friday	Viernes Santo
Easter Sunday	el Domingo de Resurrección
the April Fair in Sevilla	la Feria de Abril
the Crosses of May – celebrated in Andalucía	las Cruces de Mayo
St Fermín's day – July 7, in Pamplona	San Fermín

October 12, Our Lady of el Pilar, national day	El Pilar / Día de la Hispanidad
All Saints' Day	el día de Todos los Santos
Christmas Eve	la Nochebuena
Christmas Day	el Día de Navidad
New Year's Eve	la Nochevieja
village fête	la fiesta del pueblo / la fiesta rural
circus	el circo
concert	el concierto
band	la banda
gig	el concierto
festival of (music)	el festival (de música)
competition	la competición
championship	el campeonato
match	el partido
wine festivals....	los festivales de vino / la vendimia
national dress	el traje nacional
procession	la procesión
bullfight	la corrida de toros
bullfighter (3 roles)	el matador / el picador / el banderillero

15.5 Environmental issues

Core vocabulary

the environment	el medio ambiente
environmentalist	el ecologista
environmental issues	los asuntos medioambientales
ecology	la ecología
ecosystem	el ecosistema
erosion	la erosión
foodstuffs	los comestibles / productos alimenticios
GM (genetically modified)	alimentos transgénicos
organic	orgánico/a
artificial fertilizer	el abono / fertilizante artificial
nitrate	el nitrato
pesticide	el pesticida

poison	el veneno
weedkiller	la herbicida
pollution	la polución / contaminación
environmental pollution	la polución medioambiental
acid rain	la lluvia ácida
air pollution	la contaminación del aire / atmosférica
car exhaust	el escape del coche
detergent	el detergente
global warming	el calentamiento global
greenhouse gas	el gas invernadero
nuclear testing	las pruebas nucleares
ozone layer	la capa de ozono
radiation	la radiación
radioactive waste	los residuos radiactivos
water pollution	la polución de agua
power	la electricidad
energy	la energía
nuclear power	la energía nuclear
hydro-electric power	la energía hidroeléctrica
solar power	la energía solar
wind power	la energía del viento / eólica
power station	la central eléctrica
recycling	el reciclaje
glass, cans, paper, plastic	el vidrio, las latas, el papel, el plástico
compost	el compost
resources	los recursos
sustainable	sostenibles
renewable	renovables
the protection of the environment	la protección del medio ambiente
of animals	de los animales
of plants	de las plantas

Useful verbs

to protect	proteger
to conserve	conservar
to destroy	destruir
to dispose of	deshacerse de
to throw away	tirar

15.6 Religion

Core vocabulary

religion	la religión
beliefs	las creencias
faith	la fe
Buddhism	el budismo
Christianity	el cristianismo
Hinduism	el hinduismo
Islam	el Islam
Judaism	el Judaísmo
I am a / an	soy ...
agnostic	agnóstico
atheist	ateo
Buddhist	budista
Catholic	católico
Christian	cristiano
Hindu	hindú
Jew	judío
Moslem	musulmán
Quaker	cuáquero
Jehovah's witness	Testigo de Jehová
God	Dios
Buddha	Buda
Christ	Cristo
Mohammed	Mohama
the prophet	el profeta
cathedral	la catedral
chapel	la capilla
church	la iglesia
mosque	la mezquita
synagogue	la sinagoga
temple	el templo
religious leader	el líder religioso
bishop	el obispo
imam	el imán
monk	el monje
nun	la religiosa / la monja
priest	el sacerdote / el cura
rabbi	el rabino
prayer	la oración / el rezo
hymn	el himno

religious service	el oficio religioso
mass	la misa
baptism	el bautismo
christening	el bautizo
(first) communion	la (primera) comunión
wedding	la boda
funeral	el funeral / entierro

Useful verbs

to attend church	ir a la iglesia
to believe	creer
to pray	rezar
to preach	predicar
to kneel	arrodillarse (reflexive)
to sing	cantar
to chant	cantar
to worship	adorar

16

the media

16.1 The press

Core vocabulary

newspaper	el periódico / diario
magazine, review	la revista
comic	el cómic / tebeo / la revista de historietas
daily	diario
weekly	semanal
monthly	mensual
bi-monthly	bimensual
quarterly	trimestral
yearly	anual
publisher	la editorial
editor	el editor
journalist	el periodista
journalism	el periodismo
reporter (press)	el reportero
reporter (TV, radio)	el locutor
correspondent	el corresponsal
special correspondent	el correponsal especial
war correspondent	el corresponsal de guerra
critic	el crítico
press agency	el encargado de prensa
front page	la portada
back page	la contraportada
headline	el titular
column	la columna / sección
article	el artículo
brief report	el reportaje en breve
advertisement	el anuncio
notices	los anuncios / avisos (clasificados)
obituaries	los obituarios / las necrológicas
small ads	los anuncios por palabras

news items / *las noticias*

natural disaster	el desastre natural
flood	la inundación
earthquake	el terremoto
eruption of a volcano	la erupción de un volcán

storm	la tormenta / tempestad
hurricane	el huracán
tornado	el tornado
torrential rain	las lluvias torrenciales
road accident	el accidente de carretera / tráfico
car crash	el accidente de coche
collision	la colisión / choque
plane crash	el accidente de avión
terrorist attack	el ataque / atentado terrorista
demonstration	la manifestación
strike	la huelga
a call to go on strike	la convocatoria de huelga
fire	el incendio

- Spanish newspaper reports often use unexpected tenses; the present tense gives vividness to narration of incidents, and the imperfect is sometimes used with similar effect.
- The distinction in the British press between tabloid and broad-sheet newspapers does not exist in Spain, where most papers are the same size – smaller than a broad-sheet, but larger than a tabloid paper. There is no division of style and tone as in the UK press.
- Spanish newspapers tend focus on news rather than on celebrity gossip, which is left to magazines like *Hola*. Even regional papers contain lots of national and international news, as well as local news and information; as a result, many Spanish people buy local rather than national papers.

16.2 Books

Core vocabulary

book	el libro
title	el título
author	el autor
writer	el escritor
illustrator	el ilustrador
cartoonist	el dibujante (de dibujos animados)
paperback	el libro en rústica
biography	la biografía
autobiography	la autobiografía
novel	la novela

short story	el cuento
dictionary	el diccionario
encyclopaedia	la enciclopedia
atlas	el atlas
guide book	la guía turística
(road) map book	la guía de carreteras
fiction	la ficción
non-fiction	la literatura no novelesca

literary genres — *los géneros literarios*

novels	las novelas
mystery novels	las novelas de misterio
detective novels	las novelas policíacas
short stories	los cuentos
foreign literature	la literatura extranjera
literary review	la crítica literaria
poetry	la poesía
epics	las epopeyas / novelas épicas
essays	los ensayos

Useful verbs

to write	escribir
to edit	editar
to print	imprimir
to publish	publicar
to sign	firmar

Useful phrases

What sort of books do you like to read?	¿Qué tipo de libros te gusta leer?
Who is your favourite author?	¿Quién es tu / su autor preferido?
I like reading books about ...	Me gusta leer libros sobre ...
I like reading books where ...	Me gusta leer libros en los que ...
I like reading books that ...	Me gusta leer libros que ...

16.3 Cinema and television

Core vocabulary

the cinema	el cine

auditorium	el auditorio
(big) screen	la pantalla (grande)
seat	la silla / el asiento
foyer	el vestíbulo
ticket	la entrada
booking office	la taquilla

films — *las películas*

thriller	la película de suspense
romance	la película sentimental
love story	la historia de amor
historical film	la película de historia
science fiction	la película de ciencia ficción
horror film	la película de horror
war film	la película de guerra
comedy	la película de humor
detective film	la película policíaca
drama	la película dramática
adverts	la publicidad

the cast	el reparto / los actores
film star	una estrella de cine
actor / actress	un actor / una actriz
leading role	un papel secundario
supporting role	un papel secundario
singer	un(a) cantante
dancer	un bailarín / una bailarina
director	el director
producer	el productor
cameraman	el cámera
sound recordist	el registrador de sonido
the crew	el equipo (de cámara)

video rental / shop	el videoclub
video	el vídeo
DVD	el DVD / disco de vídeo digital

| *dubbed / subtitled* | doblado / subtitulado |

television — *la televisión*

television set	el televisor
small screen	la pantalla pequeña
cable	el cable
satellite	el satélite
dish	la antena parabólica
video recorder	el aparato de vídeo

DVD *player*	el lector (de) DVD
remote control	el mando a distancia
channel	el canal
credits	los créditos / titulares de crédito
commercials	los anuncios / spots publicitarios
cartoons	los dibujos animados
children's programmes	los programas infantiles
chat show	el programa de entrevistas
documentary	el documental
feature film	el largometraje
game show, quiz programme	el programa de concurso
news programme	el programa de actualidad
soap	la telenovela
weather forecast	el pronóstico / la previsión del tiempo / el boletín meteorológico
news reporter	el locutor
newsreader	el locutor
presenter	el presentador
interviewer	el entrevistador
commentator	el comentarista
disc jockey	el DJ / discjockey / pinchadiscos
game show host	el presentador de un programa de concurso
the viewer	el telespectador / televidente
radio	la radio
station	la emisora
programme	el programa
frequency	la frecuencia
on FM	en FM
on LW	en onda larga
on MW	en onda media

Useful verbs

to change channels	cambiar de canales
to graze / channel hop	hacer zapping
to turn on / off the telly	encender / apagar la tele
to turn the sound up	subir el volumen / poner más fuerte
to turn the sound down	reducir / bajar el volumen

to broadcast	transmitir / emitir
to record	registrar

Useful phrases

What is your favourite programme?	¿Cuál es tu programa favorito / preferido?
Do you like documentaries?	¿Te gustan los documentales?
Who is your favourite presenter?	¿Quién es tu / su presentador(a) preferido/a?
He / she is partial / impartial.	(El / ella) es parcial / imparcial.

taking it further

Books

For an introduction to Spanish history, geography, language and culture, and modern-day society, try:

Teach Yourself Spanish Language, Life and Culture, Mike Zollo and Phil Turk (Hodder & Stoughton Ltd, London, 2000).

The New Spaniards, John Hooper (Penguin, London, 1995).

Those wanting more in-depth knowledge of the language might enjoy:

How Spanish Grew, Robert K. Spaulding (University of California Press, 1967). An old but thorough text.

The History of the Spanish Language, Ralph Perry (Cambridge University Press, 1991).

The *Teach Yourself* series covers many aspects of learning Spanish, including the comprehensive *Teach Yourself Spanish* (Juan Kattán-Ibarra, Hodder & Stoughton, London, 2003), *Teach Yourself Latin American Spanish* and *Teach Yourself Spanish Grammar* – the natural partner title to this book (both titles by Juan Kattán-Ibarra, Hodder & Stoughton, London, 2003).

Watching and listening

In the UK, Televisión Española 2 and several others are available on Eutelsat FII / Hotbird on satellite television channels. Some systems can also access Hispasat, which broadcasts Spanish and Hispano–American channels. In some areas of the UK, Spanish channels are available on cable television. In the US, Spanish language TV is available in most areas.

Radio reception on a normal set in the UK is variable, though in some areas Spanish national stations can be received quite clearly, depending on atmospheric conditions. Spanish radio is available on Satellite TV.

Listen to a variety of material or programmes. Try watching or listening to the news, having already seen or heard it in the English-speaking media, as many international news items will be shown on both. This will help your understanding and give you confidence.

If you are interested in literature, particularly poetry, the work of many Spanish poets has been recorded in the form of song; CDs will be easily available in Spain, but a specialist music shop may be also able to help. Here are some suggestions:

Antonio Machado: Joan Manuel Serrat – *Dedicado a Antonio Machado* on LP or CD, comprising eleven of Machado's poems set to music, or try *Campos de Castilla*, or any anthology of Machado's poems.

Federico García Lorca: Luar na Lubre – *Chove en Santiago*, a one-poem CD, published in 1999, or try *Cabo do Mondo*, or any anthology of Lorca's poems (look for one including this poem).

Rafael Alberti: Joan Manuel Serrat – 'La Paloma' on the LP *Joan Manuel Serrat*, or any anthology of Alberti's poetry.

Many Spanish films are available on video and DVD, most with English sub-titles if you really need them!

Places to go

Look out for performances of Spanish culture in local venues, e.g. Flamenco dancing, films, South American films and music and so on. Also watch out for Spanish (speaking) films at local film clubs and on television.

Spanish paintings are sometimes displayed in galleries outside Spain, including the USA and UK; there are paintings by Velázquez in the National Gallery, London, and the National Gallery in Edinburgh.

Reading

Obviously, this will depend on whether or not you can read Spanish well enough to keep your interest going! Try short, simple items in the press, such as advertisements, small ads and short articles on well-known subjects. Another very useful source of reading material is the Internet, where there is plenty of visual material to support your understanding. Try tourist and hotel web-sites, or go to a site which deals with your hobby or your work specialization: you will already know a lot about the topic, so even understanding new words will be easier as you are familiar with the context.

If you wish to read literature in Spanish, the best approach is to go for a 'school text' if one is available, that is one which has been set for Spanish literature examinations: such editions have a useful introduction, explanatory notes and glossaries.

Websites

The web is very popular in Spain, so there is plenty of good material in Spanish available, and much also from Latin America – all good practice. Choose your subject and do the necessary search, but be prepared to be bombarded with Spanish. There are Spanish websites relating to many of the subjects covered in this book. You can either do a search using your favourite search engine, preferably one with Spanish links, or if you can cope with the language well enough to use a Spanish search engine, go direct to one of those listed below.

Be warned, that websites come and go, and their addresses often change. These were all fine at the time of going to press!

The web site address of the Spanish Embassy Education Office, the *Consejería de Educación*, is: **http://www.sgci.mec.es/uk/**

On certain specific topics the *Consejería de Educación* (Education Advisory Service) publishes booklets and work-packs in Spanish on certain subjects such as: *Las mujeres* (Women); *La juventud* (Youth); *El medio ambiente* (The environment); *La familia y las relaciones personales* (The family and personal relationships)

The Spanish Embassy in the US has an Education Office in Washington, D.C.: **http://www.sgci.mec.es/usa/**

This has some fascinating web pages in Spanish on dozens of subjects, including the Spanish Royal Family, and many other topics of current interest in Spain. Here are some further examples of Spanish government sites on specific topics:

The environment: http://www.cofis.es/medio-ambiente/

Historical information: http://www.docuweb.ca/SiSpain/ spanish/history/.html

Search for other 'official' topics on: **http://www.docuweb.ca/ SiSpain/**

Spanish Press

El País	**http://www.elpais.es**
El Mundo	**http://www.el-mundo.es/**
ABC	**http://www.abc.es/**
La Vanguardia	**http://www.vanguardia.es/**

Spanish search engines

Using a Spanish search engine may speed up your search for a specific Spanish site.

Olé	**http://www.ole.es/**
Red iris	**http://www.rediris.es/**
Directorio (LA/Spain)	**http://www.virtualizar.com/buscar/**
La Brújula (Argentina)	**http://www.brujula.com.ar/**

Language learning on the web

For basic language practice, try:

http://www.languagesonline.org.uk
http://www.bbc.co.uk/education/languages/
http://www.becta.org.uk/projects/linguanet/index.html
http://polyglot.lss.wisc.edu/lss/lang/teach.html
http://www.studyspanish.com/index.htm
http://www.geocities.com/Athens/Thebes/6177/
http://rgshw.com/index2.htm
http://www.spanishlanguage.co.uk

Try making your own word-search games to practise vocabulary, on: **http://www.makeyourownwordsearch.com**

A useful UK site for more advanced Spanish is: **http://www.sgci. mec.es/uk/Pub/tecla.html**. This site offers dozens of short articles on various topics, followed by vocabulary lists and exercises in Spanish.

Other sites offering more advanced information and practice include:
http://www.hull.ac.uk/cti/langsite.htm
http://www.well.ac.uk/

For information on the state of Spanish and links to literature, try:
http://www.el-castellano.com/

spanish
juan kattán-ibarra

- Do you want to cover the basics then progress fast?
- Have you got rusty Spanish which needs brushing up?
- Do you want to reach a high standard?

Spanish starts with the basics but moves at a lively pace to give you a good level of understanding, speaking and writing. You will have lots of opportunity to practise the kind of language you will need to be able to communicate with confidence and understand the culture of speakers of Spanish.

spanish grammar
juan kattán-ibarra

- Are you looking for an accessible guide to Spanish grammar?
- Do you want a book you can use either as a reference or as a course?
- Would you like exercises to reinforce your learning?

Spanish Grammar explains the most important structures in a clear and jargon-free way, with plenty of examples to show how they work in context. Use the book as a comprehensive reference to dip in and out of or work through it to build your knowledge.

spanish verbs
maría rosario hollis

- Do you want a handy reference guide to check verb forms?
- Are you finding tenses difficult?
- Do you want to see verbs used in a variety of contexts?

Spanish Verbs is a quick-and-easy way to check the form and meaning of over 3000 verbs. The clear layout makes the book very easy to navigate and the examples make the uses clear at the same time as building your vocabulary.

teach® yourself

Afrikaans
Arabic
Arabic Script, Beginner's
Bengali
Brazilian Portuguese
Bulgarian
Cantonese
Catalan
Chinese
Chinese, Beginner's
Chinese Language, Life & Culture
Chinese Script, Beginner's
Croatian
Czech
Danish
Dutch
Dutch, Beginner's
Dutch Dictionary
Dutch Grammar
English, American (EFL)
English as a Foreign Language
English, Correct
English Grammar
English Grammar (EFL)
English, Instant, for French Speakers
English, Instant, for German Speakers
English, Instant, for Italian Speakers
English, Instant, for Spanish Speakers
English for International Business
English Language, Life & Culture
English Verbs
English Vocabulary
Finnish
French
French, Beginner's
French Grammar
French Grammar, Quick Fix
French, Instant
French, Improve your
French Language, Life & Culture
French Starter Kit
French Verbs

French Vocabulary
Gaelic
Gaelic Dictionary
German
German, Beginner's
German Grammar
German Grammar, Quick Fix
German, Instant
German, Improve your
German Language, Life & Culture
German Verbs
German Vocabulary
Greek
Greek, Ancient
Greek, Beginner's
Greek, Instant
Greek, New Testament
Greek Script, Beginner's
Gulf Arabic
Hebrew, Biblical
Hindi
Hindi, Beginner's
Hindi Script, Beginner's
Hungarian
Icelandic
Indonesian
Irish
Italian
Italian, Beginner's
Italian Grammar
Italian Grammar, Quick Fix
Italian, Instant
Italian, Improve your
Italian Language, Life & Culture
Italian Verbs
Italian Vocabulary
Japanese
Japanese, Beginner's
Japanese, Instant
Japanese Language, Life & Culture
Japanese Script, Beginner's
Korean

Latin
Latin American Spanish
Latin, Beginner's
Latin Dictionary
Latin Grammar
Nepali
Norwegian
Panjabi
Persian, Modern
Polish
Portuguese
Portuguese, Beginner's
Portuguese Grammar
Portuguese, Instant
Portuguese Language, Life & Culture
Romanian
Russian
Russian, Beginner's
Russian Grammar
Russian, Instant
Russian Language, Life & Culture
Russian Script, Beginner's
Sanskrit
Serbian
Spanish
Spanish, Beginner's
Spanish Grammar
Spanish Grammar, Quick Fix
Spanish, Instant
Spanish, Improve your
Spanish Language, Life & Culture
Spanish Starter Kit
Spanish Verbs
Spanish Vocabulary
Swahili
Swahili Dictionary
Swedish
Tagalog
Teaching English as a Foreign Language
Teaching English One to One
Thai
Turkish
Turkish, Beginner's
Ukrainian
Urdu
Urdu Script, Beginner's
Vietnamese
Welsh
Welsh Dictionary
Welsh Language, Life & Culture
Xhosa
Zulu

available from bookshops and on-line retailers